EQUALITY AND EUROPE

EQUALITY AND EUROPE

Positive Strategies for Recruiting and Retaining Europe's Women Managers

Emery Associates

First published in September 1992
by Emery Associates
42 Downlands Road, Purley, Surrey CR8 4JE
With the assistance of Audi AG

ISBN 0 9519690 0 5

Printed in Great Britain

Bitish Library Cataloguing in Publication Data.
A catalogue record for this book is available from the British Library

HD
6054
·4
E9E63
1992

Table of Contents

PART THREE: TREATING EQUALITY AS A BUSINESS ISSUE

PART FOUR: MANAGING THE CHANGE

PART FIVE: THE BARRIERS TO EQUALITY

Foreword

Sir Derek Hornby, Chairman, The British Institute of Management

Sir Derek Hornby was made Chairman of Rank Xerox in 1984, a position he held until his recent retirement. In addition to being Chairman of the British Institute of Management, Sir Derek was appointed Chairman of the British Overseas Trade Board in 1990.

Sir Derek holds numerous directorships and is a member of Templeton College, Oxford and a patron of Oxford Management School.

Equality has become a major business issue. The First Euro Businesswoman Conference, held on March 9 and 10th 1992, at the London Hilton on Park Lane, brought together European governments, businesses and leading business academics to examine what was being done to recruit and develop more women managers. With the possible exception of Eire, most of the countries faced the same problems of static or declining population in the 1990s and emerging skill shortages - even in a recession.

As the opening speaker I was invited to look at the programme for the two days and highlight some of the things that struck me as the fundamental issues in developing a largely neglected resource - the managerial talents of women. Without their full participation in the economic life of Europe the single market will surely fail.

Opportunity 2000 - A Business-Led Initiative

On the first afternoon the conference discussed 'Opportunity 2000', a programme started recently in the UK by 61 (now 110) major companies to promote the training and employment of women in management.

Opportunity 2000 covers not only recruitment, but also career planning, management development, flexible contracts and such things as child care. It is a comprehensive, business-led programme which should show consistency of purpose and application over several years, exactly how it should be in my view. Underlying Opportunity 2000 is the need to have a consistent training and development approach in future years. I say this because when I was working with Rank Xerox Corporation in the 1970s in America, Xerox, in conjunction with a number of other companies, was involved in applying the principles of the US Federal Government's Affirmative Action (equal opportunities) Programme. As a result there was an upsurge of women in managerial and technical posts over the next five or six years.

It was extremely tough to introduce and manage the programme which caused considerable friction and tension, because there was obviously some positive discrimination involved. It was also perceived as quite unfair and disruptive to the company as a whole. Yet it achieved its objective. I am hoping that the Opportunity 2000's approach will achieve those same objectives but in a less divisive way.

New Work Patterns

The second major issue I highlighted was new work patterns. These offer major opportunities. Over the last few years companies, especially those involved in international competition, have had to learn to do business in different ways.

A few years ago it became obvious that Xerox was not going to be able to compete against the Japanese, with its existing organisation structure. We had a very large central staff operation with resources and support services at a level we could not maintain. One of the things that emerged from our deliberations - mainly from among the employees themselves - was that it was possible to continue to work for a company without a contract of service, without working a forty hour week and without coming to work every day.

Indeed, the very products that we were making at that time - workstations and faxes - made it possible for people to work and do the tasks that they had carried out in the past but in entirely different ways, often at their own discretion.

In a similar vein some of you will be aware what Steve Shirley running a company called 'F International' achieved in the 1970s and 1980s.

Working for ICL in the 1970s, Steve fell pregnant and was asked to leave. Having done so she got a few friends around her and started a software company at home, staffed by women who were in the same situation as herself. Almost unwittingly, Steve had discovered the perfect career path for herself and those around her. Women worked for her in their own homes writing software through the initial period of their children's education, and then progressed to handling field management jobs as their family responsibilities lessened.

Steve developed that company from four people in 1968 to the 2,500-3,000 people it is today with a turnover of £25 million. During that time she pioneered patterns of work previously unknown. I think that these will become increasingly familiar as they offer not only women, but everyone a major opportunity.

Dramatic Changes in Management

My final observation concerned managerial change. In the UK the organisational structures of companies have changed radically. Today, something like 90% of UK companies employ less than 200 people. We have had to focus on international competition and the customer, like never before. The emergence of Total Quality Training has created fundamental changes, not only in British industry but also European.

People have now learnt to work together in teams, not just up and down a chain of command. This has been difficult for the traditional manager to accept. Used to managing through a hierarchy, it has been uncomfortable to have training programmes that encourage people to work together, and not through a manager. It has really changed the manager's job and his skills.

I regarded this as a very important gathering and I hope that this volume of proceedings will achieve a very wide circulation, as a comprehensive assessment and guide of what Europe is doing and needs to do, to dramatically increase women's contribution to economic life, and ultimately to empower all sections of the workforce to utilise their abilities to the full.

Acknowledgements

Emery Associates would like to express its thanks and appreciation to everyone who has contributed to the holding of the conference and this publication.

We would like to thank the following in particular:

Audi AG for sponsoring this publication.

The European for helping us to launch the original concept, especially journalist Tessa Thomas and the continuing support of the Art Desk under the skilful direction of David Wadmore.

The Equal Opportunities Unit of the European Commission, headed by Agnes Hubert, for sponsoring the overseas speakers.

The Daily Telegraph for its editorial and advertising support and the Phyllida Onslow of the Telegraph's Marketing Department.

All the speakers and panellists.

Our two excellent chairpersons, Sue MacGregor OBE and Professor Peter Herriot of Sundridge Park Management College.

Everyone who helped in any way with the organisation and management of the conference and putting together this publication; in particular: Carole Pemberton, Lesley Abdela, Maryline Colin, Dorothy Emery, Jenny Riley, John Cook and Paul Treseder.

INTRODUCTION

Equality and the European Market

Equality and the European Market

Joanna Foster, Chair, UK Equal Opportunities Commission, President, EC's Advisory Committee on Equal Opportunities.

Joanna Foster worked at Insead Business School at Fontainbleau and has also directed change management programmes for famiiies and companies at the University of Pittsburgh, USA.

Prior to joining the Equal Opportunites Commission, Joanna Foster was head of the Pepperell Unit at the Industrial Society. Joanna took over the EC Advisory Committee Chair in 1992.

The aim of this conference is to see what industry can do to ensure it attracts and retains a much higher proportion of its female management potential.

My aim in this session is to underline what we need to be doing both on a pan-European basis, and as individual member countries to help make this happen. Bringing down the economic barriers to develop the single market is Europe's response to increasingly fierce international competition.

Exploiting the Imagination and Creativity of the Individual

As the economic barriers come down, the challenge for each country, each government, each employer, each trade union and each educator is to set alight the imagination and innovation and creativity of every individual European; to mobilise the energy and to motivate both women and men to contribute their skills and ideas. To do this the social barriers have to come down as well. This is the challenge for Europe as a whole, including us here in the UK. To succeed we have to produce a high added value/high skill economy which can out perform in the markets currently dominated by the USA, Japan and other Pacific Rim countries.

To do this we have to change not just by altering the rules and regulations that govern the free movement of goods, services and people across national boundaries, but also our attitudes about how we treat and develop our people. In particular, industry and business helped by the leadership and the framework established by Government, have to start tackling seriously the barriers both in the mind and those encountered everyday by half the population - women.

Here in the UK more than half of this year's entrants to university and college are women, and over half the qualifying lawyers, doctors and accountants are now women. Yet, as we are all aware, women are still sparsely represented in the senior echelons of business and the professions, despite the steady but still slow increase in the numbers of women middle managers. The same applies to almost every area of decision-making in this country.

European business needs women and European women need business. Economic necessity as well as aspiration combine to make the numbers of women now in the labour force greater than ever before in every Community country. The demographic gap and the skills gap underline the future imperative for urgent action to get women out of the low pay, low status jobs and to integrate them properly into the workforce, into quality full time or part time jobs that have real prospects, decent protection, decent benefits, pay and training. Into jobs where being a parent or carer of an elderly or dependent relative is not penalised,

4

but valued, along with professional skills. Only then will Europe be well placed to pit its brain power and creativity against the rest of the world.

Equal Opportunities and the Role of the Community

The European Community has played a pivotal role in promoting equality of opportunities between women and men. Equal Treatment is enshrined in Article 119 of the Treaty of Rome. Since 1975, following the adoption of the Social Action Programme, the Community, both through its legislative programme and through its equal opportunity action programmes, has significantly influenced the development of equal opportunities in our respective member countries.

Here in the UK its impact is enormous. Julie Hayward in her landmark equal value case, Douglas Barber in his pensions case, and Helen Marshall in her equal retirement age case are key examples. And there are many more women who will benefit if the EOC wins its judicial review appeal proceedings against the British Government on conditions for part-time workers.

Nevertheless there is still a long way to go, and the single market, while it promises economic opportunities for some, certainly does not promise equal opportunities for all. At our last Advisory Committee meeting in Brussels in January, there was universal concern about the future prospects for women's employment and economic situation. 'Vulnerable' was the word we used.

The Third Action Programme for Equal Opportunities

Anticipating the enormous changes facing Europe in the 1990s, the European Commission's Third Action Programme for Equal Opportunities, which was adopted last year, emphasises action and partnership. It was developed and backed by all the major players in the European equality field: for instance, the Equality Unit at the Commission, with its European and national networks of equality experts; the Advisory Committee for Equal Opportunities where I regularly meet my counterparts from other agencies, and the European employer and trade union representatives; and the Womens' Committee of the European Parliament and the European Womens' Lobby.

The Third Action Programme highlights three priority areas:

— The application and further development of European Community equality laws.

— The integration of women securely into the workforce with emphasis on helping women and men balance their work and family responsibilities, on education and training, and on pay

— Improving the status of women in society, including getting more women into decision-making jobs

The programme has now been launched in each country and in the course of the next four years there will be an evaluation of how each country is doing. Alongside this programme the European Commission's social policy programme continues to bring forward measures to advance equal opportunities. Current initiatives include the Recommendation on the dignity of women and men at work with its excellent Code of Good Practice on sexual harassment developed by Michael Rubinstein. Breaking through glass ceilings is about changing the culture as well as changing outdated practices, and this code spells out in a commonsense way how the environment at work can be improved. I very much welcome the Employment Department's launch last week of an excellent publication on sexual harassment aimed at British employers.

In December the Council of Ministers adopted the European Commission's draft Recommendation on Child care produced by Peter Moss and his Child care Network. Like the key to real choice; an Action Plan for Child care which we produced at the Equal Opportunities Commission last year, the Recommendation advocates a partnership policy with employers and parents, with Government taking a leading and co-ordinating role, especially when it comes to funding.

Two other very relevant Directives are current. One is the Maternity Directive, and the other the Working Time Directive. If adopted, both would have major impact on the lives of working women and their families. Unfortunately the Maternity Directive as it now stands is a feeble, watered-down version of what it should be. For example, the draft text equates pregnancy with sickness. My colleagues and I in the Advisory Committee and at the EOC find this offensive and reject this concept. We are pushing for an amendment to recognise pregnancy as a separate and different condition, needing appropriate and distinct provision for pay and entitlements.

Long Working Hours Pressurise Families

On the organisation of working time, I would just like to say that in our recent research survey, Working Time, the EOC found that it was clear that something has to change our patterns of work. Due to their pay and bonus systems, men in the UK work the longest hours in Europe, and women work all sorts of hours in part-time jobs from pre-dawn to twilight shifts. No wonder families are under pressure.

Other Directives on parental and family leave will address this issue, and in the post-Maastricht era of the new social chapter we shall watch with keen interest to see what commitment the British government shows in backing these initiatives.

At the EOC we have published our agenda for action - our Equality Agenda. What women want in this country is a fair deal at work, and child care. During our imminent General Election we will be asking each party what they will do for equal opportunities - whether they will accept the EOC's proposals to amend the equality legislation which is now rusty, complex, costly and inconsistent with European law; what they will do for part-timers; what they will do about pensions; about fair pay; about pregnancy provision, paternity and maternity leave; about training for women; and most of all, about what they will do to provide families with affordable, quality child care.

I hope the debate in the coming weeks will focus on what sort of Britain within Europe we want. If we want the single Europe to succeed, we need a quality workforce. Some governments, businesses and individuals will need pushing, and for that we need the law. Others will recognise their own self-interest and will move ahead. But above all they will understand that equality is also treating all our people fairly.

PART ONE

Economic and Social Change Favours Women

Women and the European Labour Market

Richard Pearson, Director, The Institute Of Manpower Studies.

Richard Pearson was appointed Director of the Institute of Manpower Studies in 1992. An economist, Richard Pearson has published and lectured widely.

The IMS is an international independent research body which has an extensive work programme related to equal opportunities and the employment of women.

The Institute of Manpower Studies is an independent international research institute focusing on human resource issues and works in the corporate and the public sectors. It works to very specific programmes within organisations: including human resource development, employment policy, career planning, equal opportunities and flows within the international labour market.

Today I want to reflect on the position of women in a European labour market which is changing in ways which I believe will be mainly, but not wholly, beneficial to them.

However, initially I will talk about the labour market in general. I will be examining changing job patterns, how European employers are responding and then highlight the ways in which these affect women.

The Issues Facing Employers And The Labour Market

Looking at the issues facing the labour market and employers in the 1990s, I identified five that had a bearing on human resources.

The most pertinent is the current recession in the UK and Europe, now becoming worldwide. It poses two main challenges. The first and most obvious is to bring it to an end as quickly as possible, and move back onto the growth curve. Second, if we are actually planning for a more prosperous future, how can we bring this about, and what are the human resources that will help us to grow our economies and societies?

I do not think a convincing argument has yet been made that growth per se is environmentally damaging. Certain aspects are, but I believe we can still grow our economies considerably. We can be more wealthy, better housed and looked after without damaging our fellows or the environment. Within the UK and within Europe we have to ask what is possible.

We tell ourselves that we are in a prosperous European labour market and economy and yet it is not prosperous relative to some of our major competitors. If we look at economic growth in Japan during the 1980s it achieved 4% per annum. In the United States, the stagnant USA, it was two and a half per cent; yet in the European Community it was under 2%.

If we look at Europe's wealth prospects then the Americans are still over 50% more affluent per head, with the Japanese rather less so at 12%. These should be regarded as reference points, indicating what can be achieved.

Even within Europe wealth remains relative. Germany, Luxembourg and Denmark - the richest nations within the European Community - have wealth levels some 25% above the average. At the other extreme - Ireland, Spain Greece and Portugal - we are talking about 50-70% of the average. These are rather crude numbers but they show a very varied economic picture within Europe.

The issue for the UK today and in the future is how do we want to compete in Europe? Do want to be a high wage, high prosperity economy or do we want to compete on low wages. We really have no option since I believe none of us wants to try and compete as a low wage economy against the emerging Eastern European and Far Eastern economies. UK wages could be cut and re-cut but still not be economic on a per hour basis with the rest of the world.

We need to be a high wage, high productivity economy with high value-added activities, using and investing in our human resources more effectively.

We have to look to technology to help us, which is one of our of main challenges in the nineties. Technology has cut a swathe through the manufacturing and primary industries. It is only just beginning to touch the service sector, although most of us here can already see it sitting on our desks - a thing we would not have dreamt of a decade ago. Many new skills are still required, even though skill shortages as such have dropped out of the headlines over the last year or so.

Skill Shortages Are Selective

Europe remains an ill-defined place. Although the bureaucrats tell us it is a community of twelve nations, reality is much more blurred since we have other trading relationships with the EFTA States and an increasing involvement with Eastern Europe.

If we go back a couple of years, skill shortages were constraining developments in France, Germany prior to reunification, Belgium, the Netherlands and here in the UK. But they were selective. They were predominantly higher level skills - marketing, sales, management and finance - areas where women in particular are making the most inroads. Indeed, one of the challenges for employers in the future is to unlock the potential of the people they already have.

We have heard a lot about the 'demographic time bomb' and I will refer to it again, but it is important to bear in mind that we are an ageing society. We had half a million new entrants to the Community workforce in the 1970s. In 1991 it was about two thousand across the whole of Europe, allowing for those coming and going. By the end of the century our workforce will be declining! As the population growth continues to decline a smaller workforce will have to support more people. To reiterate, it will be a major challenge to use that human resource more effectively.

The Real Impact Of 1992 On Business

What will be the real impact of 1992 on business? Well of course 1992 is already upon us. 1993 is actually what it's all about because that is when the single European market officially comes into being. I would argue that it is primarily an economic and attitudinal issue. It will have little direct impact on employment. After all, in reality, unconstrained mobility of labour already exists, although still restricted in Spain and Portugal in some respects until 1994. Perhaps the most important thing coming out of 1993 for employment, although its impact will be uneven, is the Social Charter. In policy terms at least it promises to be very supportive of equal opportunities programmes - a major Community initiative.

I think the biggest change we are seeing concerning 1992 - actually a follow-on from the media campaigns and advertising - is symbolism. Increasingly we are seeing ourselves as 'Europeans', not French, Germans, or Britons and if you look at the results of surveys, particularly of young people, you will find that they see themselves operating increasingly within a European framework. This may be idealised. In reality most will stay within their own communities and national borders. But people are increasingly thinking European. For example, last year 65% of British undergraduates said they wanted to work elsewhere in Europe at some stage in their careers.

Will Mobility Increase?

And so to mobility. Are we all going to rush around Europe in 1993 and swap jobs? I would argue not. First of all 1993 does not make any differences because the work permit is not a problem. Indeed, since the Community was formed, mobility within Europe has actually declined. There are actually less people moving around Europe now than there were 20 years ago, when the initial flows were from the poor to the rich countries. What we are seeing now is a growth in mobility among professional groups, and I will come back to some of the jobs most affected.

It is important just to touch briefly on some of the changes that we see within Europe, although, as I said earlier, significant differences exist between member states. Unemployment ranges from 18-20% in countries like Ireland and Spain, to much lower levels in places like the UK and Germany. Indeed, the UK has one of lowest unemployment rates in Europe at 6-8%. But concern is growing in Brussels and the Community that gradually we are reverting to a 1970s agenda - one of long-term unemployment at the unskilled end of the market.

Male Dominated Primary Industries Are in Decline

When talking about growth I think we have to recognise an increasingly fragmented labour market. We also need to understand and recognise the way that industry and the commerce are changing. Currently we are seeing the long term decline of primary industries like oil, manufacturing or coal - with their heavy preponderance of male manual workers, professionals and managers. The main growth is in the service sectors: financial, retailing, health, education, tourism, and leisure. All 'women friendly' - terrible jargon - sectors where women already have higher levels of representation compared to others. The other important factor whether a job seeker, or an employer, is not the sector you're in, because increasingly these are ill-defined, but the types of people you employ.

I won't pretend that we know for certain what is going to happen in the future - but, assuming the economy returns to its long term growth curve at about 2%, we will see the number of jobs growing. The important thing is that the fastest growing occupations are for managers, scientists, engineers and 'other professionals', a clumsy way of describing marketing, accountancy. etc. Also required are associate professionals at a technician level - health workers for example. These are the growth occupations in the 1990s. Similar trends can be seen in Germany, France, the UK and the United States - the developed economies.

15

The Good News For Businesswomen

For the European businesswoman the good news is that these are areas where equal opportunities are also the best developed, and where the economic need for new and better skills is the strongest! We can also see stagnation in demand for some skilled manual occupations, and a decline in the unskilled and other categories. So we see the market moving towards a more 'women friendly' occupational structure over time.

If we look at other aspects of change, how are employers responding? There is always organisational change, to some extent there is a fashion - decentralisation versus centralisation - currently we are going through a strong wave of decentralisation, 'small is beautiful', focusing on markets and on the individual.

This has two implications. One is making the labour market more flexible in terms of having more smaller businesses. This is a potential disadvantage to women. If you look at where positive action and equal opportunities programmes are strongest they tend to be in the big institutionalised employers, e.g. the banks and the public sector. These organisations are currently breaking-up into smaller units where the discretion and the management control is going far more to line managers.

Equal Opportunities Make Business Sense

The issue is then to educate these line managers to want equal opportunities - not because its a good thing, or society says so; nor because it's fair, but because it brings competitive advantages and is an economic necessity. This is the way we see equal opportunities programmes progressing more quickly.

We can also see some other changes in terms of employment relationships. Increasingly important, we see a growth in what we dub the 'peripheral workforce' i.e. temporary and casual workers, and to a very limited extent teleworkers - all employment relationships predominantly entered into by women. Although recognising this flexibility is often imposed upon them by domestic or other constraints, women have already adapted. The downside of these changes is that they are predominantly in lower-paid activities.

A major challenge has been selling part-time working at managerial level. There is a big debate about the feasibility of managing a company on a part-time basis. Well, if the part-time element is small enough the answer is "yes" - the chairman of many a big company is a director of fifteen others - clearly sixteen part time jobs! Now we have to dissect that argument somewhat before we take it too far. But certainly flexibility is appearing at the lower end of the labour market.

Empowering The Individual

Another important aspect of changing employment relationships is related to what one might call "personnel decentralisation". There is an increasing trend towards empowering the individual. As an outcome of this employing organisations now say "we can't plan your career, we don't know where we'll be in five or ten years, we don't know where we'll be next year!" So how can we say: "oh yes, stay with us now, we are a big multinational company and in two years time you'll be going to Venezuela, and two years after that to Paris", etc.

Increasingly companies are saying "you are our key resource, we will develop you, we'll train you, we will give you career advice and counselling, we'll give you assessment centres to see where your best potential is. As an employer we need to have a pool of good resource people, and when opportunities come up in two years time we can call on that resource". The opportunity for the individual, particularly for the businesswoman, is to say "this is how I want to map my career", rather than following a stereotyped, rather macho model, where you are expected to pick up house at twenty-four hours notice and go to the other end of Europe, or the world.

Employment Will Stay Localised

I have already touched upon the fact that mobility is growing within the Community at a professional level. But our research with employers shows that the vast majority of employment will still continue to be organised on a local basis. You won't be an employee in the

17

UK, you'll be an employee in London, Brighton or Manchester. You won't be an employee in Europe, you'll be based in Lyons, and that is where your career is likely to stay for the vast majority of people. I would argue this a good sign for women who, by and large, are less mobile than men - predominantly because of their domestic roles. So the continued emphasis of most employers, and most job resourcing at a local level, will be either beneficial or at least not disadvantageous to women.

Having said this, of course the important thing is to remember that childcare is not specifically a woman's problem, but a parent's problem, and one of the things that has got to be done quickly is to actually shift responsibility from women to parents to start bringing about changes.

We have also looked at which labour markets are the most mobile within Europe. We found job market becoming 'Europeanised' in four areas:-

Number one is top managers and the main boards of the very big companies. A small, very rarefied group with access difficult to men, and even more so for women and this is an area that I will not spend a lot of time on.

Number two are specialists operating in the European market, many locked into the traditionally male-dominated occupations of science, technology and engineering where women are numerically under-represented, although we are seeing occupations such as marketing and finance becoming increasingly Europeanised.

The third group within the corporate sector is related to management development, with individuals being moved around for experience within Europe. It is a 'good thing' to have worked in another country, and it is a good thing to have multinational management teams. The issue for women here is how geographically mobile they are, although the problems are actually increasingly non-gender specific because, with today's dual careers, the major question is more likely to be whose career comes first.

I think a major challenge for employers is how to create the degree of mobility they would like, an international management cadre, without actually uprooting the whole workforce and becoming an expatriate organisation.

In the fourth group we identified, there were some glimmerings of graduate recruitment across Europe. French companies recruiting here, British companies recruiting in Germany, and so on. While there is a lot of hype about this, our research shows it is still at a very low level. Only 50 British companies recruited new graduates from outside the UK in the last four years. Rather fewer companies came to the UK to recruit. So I think in the graduate market more of the change will be driven by the individual knocking on doors, and saying "I want to work here".

Labour Availability - The Employer's Perspective

I touched on the demand side. How is the availability of people going to change from the employer's perspective?

I think everyone knows about the demographic time bomb. You have read about it. It has not gone away. The stark figures show that, in what was West Germany, the number of young people drops by 45% in the mid-nineties; in Italy and the UK it declines by 35% and in America. Figures elsewhere in Europe are comparable.

So we see a tightening of the market, less young people coming in and more attention going to the better utilisation of existing staff. There will be major initiatives to invest in education - not just up to the ages of eighteen and twenty-one. Women participate on an equal basis with men in terms of how long they stay in education, but the subjects they study will remain very different. Women still read the arts and social sciences predominantly, which will continue to limit their opportunities, and the way in which they can be employed in the future.

Making Better Use Of What We Have

In terms of female participation in the workforce there is a very variable picture across Europe. Denmark has the highest proportion of women working. You could say this is either a good or a bad trend because it means we cannot get many more women into the labour market, giving us a very tight labour situation to start with. Again this means making better use of our existing resources of people.

In the UK we have a very high activity rate for women participating in the labour market The problem, as in the rest of Europe and North America, is that women are segmented into certain industries and occupations. They are in the services, which is good because they are in the growth sectors, but the occupations concerned tend to be at the bottom end of the market.

Also if women are involved at a professional and managerial level, they are more likely to be in the administrative and support functions than line management, where the key role models still remain for executive positions.

What Does It All Mean For Women?

To summarise, on the supply side we see a shrinking labour market/static numbers, less young people, with women as one of the key resources to be tapped into. I also touched on mobility. I don't need to remind you about the barriers to mobility which will reinforce a localised, domestic employment pattern which again I would argue is advantageous to women.

In essence what does the changing European labour market mean for women?

Well, we have looked at the growth of new jobs and the service sector - supposedly women friendly - and I think this is predominantly good news. We see labour demand in Europe's developed northern economies converging. For example, the need for marketing skills is becoming increasingly common across Europe, and at a high level. So, opportunities for women will continue to grow on a European basis. The issue for women is, can they take advantage of this demand surge by becoming more mobile?

Skill shortages are expected to recur as soon as the economy starts to pick up, there being no signs that anything structural has been done to take skill shortages off the agenda. Indeed, demographic effects are going to exacerbate them in the mid 1990s.

We have new working patterns, we have employers becoming increasingly decentralised, managers taking more control, more part-time working, more temporary working, more self-employment; all job patterns that women have traditionally had to adapt to. The issue is how far these models will apply at a professional and managerial level - not a problem in theory, but in practice a barrier to break down.

We will see increasing complexity and variability within the European labour market. We can't actually talk about a 'European' labour market as such and I don't think we can talk either about blanket equal opportunities policies or blanket solutions for women.

Increasingly work roles will be based on individualised packages. We each need to learn from each other what works best and where and how to bring about change.

Finally, we must remember the two main challenges. One is to change the new entrants coming into the market - our young people, our graduates entering the labour market for the first time. I think their equal opportunities will be much more of a reality.

But that reality will still take twenty years to move them into senior management and top professional positions. It is a process which will take a long time to effect change. So we must not neglect our existing pool of people, and this is where our second major challenge now lies. There are a lot of skills, a lot of untapped potential. How we unlock it is our challenge for the future, and I hope we can identify some of the solutions today and tomorrow.

The Best Managerial Qualities
are Feminine

Francis Kinsman, Futurist, Consultant, Journalist and Lecturer

Francis Kinsman worked in the City of London in a variety of financial service positions before going freelance in 1972.

A futurist, Francis Kinsman is an expert in the impact of social change on business and management and is also an experienced broadcaster, public speaker, lecturer and writer, having contributed a regular column to the Times.

Most managers are still too cautious or too greedy to risk the scrupulousness, openness, and imagination that will be vital to business success as we approach the new Millennium. As yet, they fail to recognise the fact that Something Else is Going On. This Something is the emergence of a whole new 'post-industrial' philosophy, miles from the 'industrial' and 'agrarian' value systems that have preceded it. Opinion research reveals that some 85% of the population of the West belongs to one, or other of three invisible 'clubs', and that the clubs themselves are of roughly equal strength and muscle in this country. Social turbulence is in the offing.

The Three Invisible Clubs

First, and familiar to most of us, the 'agrarian', or sustenance driven group is concerned with maintaining the status quo. It is change-averse, risk-averse, tribal, stable, class conscious, and nostalgic. Its mainspring is the dependency culture, both for those who depend, and those who are depended upon.

In contrast, an 'industrial' philosophy is what characterises the outer directed group. Their vision is focused outwards, always looking to see the impact they are making. It is a world of competition, aggression, materialism, thrust, discovery, glitz, cleverness and independence. Their world contains not only the yuppies and the tycoons but also the assistant sales manager's wife, ogling the Chairman at the company dance in order to secure her husband's promotion.

Finally there are the 'post-industrial' inner directeds, who are largely responsible for the green revolution we are now experiencing. Their demands are not only for conserving the environment, however, but also about conserving the people who inhabit it; for their self-fulfilment, self-development, and personal empowerment. Health and education, openness and autonomy, interdependence and a human scale for all human activities are their concerns. They are growing fast, but hard to pin down. Prince Charles is their unofficial spokesman. The others call them 'wimps'.

This is, of course, a vastly over-simplified picture. All developed societies exhibit these divisions, but their proportions differ widely by country, as do the national sub-divisions into which the three main groups are split. However, regular opinion research in 17 different countries since 1973 is backed by both established psychological theory and media evidence, here. There is strong support for the basic premise of a society divided into three philosophical parts, rather than the traditional two of 'Us' and 'Them'; with the third, inner directed group now making much of the running.

The Implications for Business

Business must now understand the nature of the inner directeds as consumers, as investors, as employees and as representing the public at large. Some organisations are getting the message; for a role model you need look no further than The Body Shop, successful in everything it touches, and faithful to the principles of imaginatively decent conduct. Businesses that follow this path are not only going to 'do well by doing good', they are going to provide the mainspring for the regeneration of the whole planet.

Meanwhile it is in the work place and within the organisation that some of the most interesting results of this shift in values are being seen. Masked somewhat by the recession, there is nonetheless a strong bias among both graduate entrants and middle managers to vote with their feet in favour of green, ethical employers and against the cynical waste-layers. Structures are becoming flatter and less bureaucratic, with project driven teams working on a circular command basis. The masculine shape of the organisation tree is out, the softer outline of the 'organisation sponge' is in; many units working semi-independently, connected to each other by a stable matrix which supports them and is nourished by their activities.

Networking - or what men call gossip when women do it among themselves - takes place as a matter of course within and between such organisations, particularly those with an international flavour. Experiments with flexible working methods - as to time, place, information handling and human inter-relationships - are proliferating in this climate. More flexible, too, are attitudes towards personal growth and fulfilment, with work coming to be seen as a crucial aspect of the whole person's process, but by no means always the one that imposes the most powerful imperatives.

The Best Management Qualities Are Feminine

All this demands an increasing commitment to care and concern by managers; it is coming to the stage where the best management has qualities that could be labelled as feminine ones. However, it is also a fact that the most unusually successful military units, such as the SAS, have always relied on this sense of 'family' and total mutual support, while the most incompetent have resorted to petty regulation and bureaucracy. So the new, millennial, organisation embodies -

- Leadership from alongside, not from above; which says "come here", rather than "go there".

- Open teamwork where all strengths and weaknesses are recognised and accepted by both the individual and the collective.

- Recognition of the value of intuition, humour, allegory and metaphor in the creative management process.

European Recruitment and Women

Ken Davidson, Vice-President, Manpower Europe

Ken Davidson is a Vice President of Manpower Inc., the world's largest employment services company with 2,550 offices in 34 countries. He now focuses on the European operations of Manpower and the implications of 1993.

Ken Davidson is keenly interested in teleworking - a practice he has pioneered in Manpower Europe.

With a network of offices across Europe and an enormous customer base, Manpower has a unique perspective on what the market is thinking and planning.

I want to talk about what is is happening on the European recruitment scene, which transferrable skills are, and maybe, in demand and finally, how rapidly job mobility could increase within the single market.

I will finish with some brief thoughts for Euro-recruiters and Euro-jobhunters.

European Recruitment Scene

In general, our customers across Europe are saying that they anticipate difficulties in recruitment at nearly all levels. They also recognise quite clearly that they will be competing for scarce resources.

In our experience, the human resources professionals in our customer base are very aware of their national and the general European demographic data, and they are very concerned about its implications. Therefore it is being regarded as a highly strategic issue, which will call for creative solutions to be applied.

The good news is that there is a clear acceptance that women will be part of the solution. Their challenge will probably be to convice others. The data does speak for itself. In Europe, women now make up more than 40% of graduates in business, economics and law. They still wait to be encouraged or enticed into engineering and natural sciences in larger numbers, but they are gradually gaining critical mass.

You are probably aware that at an executive and professional level there are differences between countries in the preferred methods of recruitment. This means that UK recruiters looking to other countries as skill sources should not assume that what works best for them in the UK will be equally effective, or indeed appropriate, in mainland Europe.

UK recruiters and foreign English-speaking recruiters may find it helpful to refer to a comprehensive and current reference guide to recruitment in Europe in a book published by the UK Institute of Personnel Management as part of its series of European Management Guides. It is called quite simply 'Recruitment'. This publication would also be a great help to job hunters who are considering looking for positions outside their home countries.

Demand For Transferrable Skills

In most countries there is a shortage of data processing or information technology specialists. In these cases UK nationals do have an advantage because, as in air traffic control, English is the official language.

Generally speaking, marketing skills are both transportable and in demand. Professionals with international knowledge of their subject: accountants, lawyers and human resources specialists are and will continue to be in demand. Everywhere there is a shortage of qualified engineers who are courted and cossetted whenever they can be found.

Looking ahead, as Europe moves from recessionary or simply sluggish economies, this demand will rise and companies will compete increasingly fiercely across international boundaries to find, attract and retain people with these sought after skills.

However, with the exception of air traffic controllers and information technology types, there is one major snag. People will only be effective in another country if they speak the language. After all, I think it is generally accepted that the best language is always the language of the customer.

It is much more likely therefore that UK recruiters will go hunting for the scarce skills in mainland Europe where there is a much greater multilingual tradition. The problem is that the UK simply does not produce enough multilingual professionals. The UK education system is incredibly short-sighted in not taking active steps to encourage multilingual ability.

This short-sightedness means that the UK workforce of the future is being placed at an increasing disadvantage compared with their European compatriots.

Speed Of Job Mobility

Transferrable skills also imply job mobility, but what degree of mobility and are we likely to see more generally?

If you recall, the UK has had a history of considerable regional skill imbalances in one part of the country with jobs available in another. There was almost a complete failure to match them up for a variety of reasons. Lack of accommodation or its high cost at the new work site were cited as factors. A reluctance to uproot families was another. Other countries have experienced much the same, so in the short term I am not optimistic about seeing substantial mobility at worker and skilled worker levels. Quite frankly, it would be a great benefit to the core business of Manpower if this were to happen but, as I just said, I am pessimistic.

We are much more likely to see mobility at management and professional levels, where progress towards the mutual recognition of qualifications by different countries in the European Community is quite advanced.

Cross-border recruiters will know however that there are a number of complex factors to be considered. The mobility considerations of managers and professionals are very different from that of the general worker and technician groups. Factors such as challenge, opportunity, quality of life, spending or buying power - not necessarily gross income - are all important to varying degrees. There are wide variations in social benefits and job protection across Europe which have yet to be harmonised' and salary levels have significant country-to-country variances.

However, I strongly believe that language is the main lubricant of mobility, and I predict that UK nationals will lose out to its more linguistically versatile neighbours. It could even be argued that in the UK there is a largely unrecognised, or certainly unacknowledged, crisis situation developing with very significant long-term implications.

In past crisis situations, government's response has been to appoint a special Minister. (Did the UK not once have a Minister for Drought?) Right now the UK's foreign language sources run at a trickle. Maybe we should have a Minister for Languages to divine for more sources. We could even have great fun with a competition for the departmental logo, possibly a combination of a dowsing rod and a tongue. Seriously, it is a significant problem and I hope that resources will be applied to providing a solution.

In the past few minutes, I have talked briefly and indeed fairly superficially about recruitment in Europe, transferrable skills and the outlook for job mobility. My comments reflect perceptions arising from the experience of Manpower's European network, plus a few personal observations and concerns.

When I began I said that I would close with some brief thoughts for recruiters and job hunters. So, let's address job hunters first. As you have already heard, there are differences between countries in recruitment and job-finding methods, quite substantial in some cases. There is however one method which is common to all. It's not particularly new, it has simply been branded and given a higher profile. It is of course 'networking'.

You may be interested to know that analysis suggests that something in the order of one third of all positions are filled from a contact or recommendation of some kind being involved. It is therefore a technique that can have immense value. So, despite the fact that it can be a very frustrating experience, it is a method of job hunting that should not be ignored' and remember, even though potentially hundreds of calls might have to be made, it only takes one to work at the end of the day!

What Is Networking In The Context Of Job Hunting?

Essentially, it is seeking to maximise upon all the contacts and friends that you have made, either socially or in the course of your business career - with a view to achieving any of a number of objectives. You could be:

—   Alerting that individual to your position and the sort of thing that you are looking for.

—   Ascertaining whether that particular individual knows of anything specifically that could be of interest.

—   Spreading the net by obtaining the names of some additional people to whom that person feels it might be worth talking.

—   Keeping abreast of general developments within, perhaps,the job market as a whole, your own field in particular, market gossip, etc.

As an example, your network of contacts could be made up of business acquaintances, colleagues, customers, competitors, recruiters, relatives, friends etc. Maybe even the odd enemy!

Now, this is not the forum for discussing the detailed methodology and courtesies of networking as a positive business tool. If anyone wants more information I can provide impeccable sources later.

Turning to recruiters, as you probably know, executive search and selection organisations have been busy expanding their direct or associate contacts throughout Europe, in anticipation of an increase in demand for what is being called the 'Euro-executive'. Inevitably they will be a resource that you may wish to use because they do have good access to the market.

For example, recently I gave an assignment to such an organisation in Germany, and I was intrigued by the lack of women among the candidates. When I challenged the consultant about this he indicated that it was just a matter of time before women would reach the levels in Germany which would have put them on my candidate list. He also told me that his firm was tracking 250 women MBAs in Germany alone, so you can see that the participation rate of women in executive positions is beginning to rise albeit fairly slowly.

However, my final hint to recruiters is precisely the same as that given to the job hunters - network. I hope you are not disappointed and see this as being oversimplistic. The reason it makes sense is because one is the mirror image of the other. Recruiters have a job to fill, job seekers are looking for one. I hope you find each other.

Will the Future 'Euro-Manager' be Genderless?

Dr Zoltan Szemerey, Deputy Director,
Asea Brown Boveri Power Ventures, Zurich

Dr Szemerey kindly delivered this address on behalf of Barbara Kux, President of ABB Power Ventures, Zurich.

Barbara Kux received her MBA from INSEAD and spent five years working in Germany for McKinsey & Co Inc. prior to joining ABB in 1989 as Vice President, ABB Zurich.

Promoted to President, Barbara Kux is currently managing five joint power ventures in Eastern Europe.

The need to develop 'Euro-managers' stems from the challenges companies are now facing in Europe and elsewhere in the world.

What are these challenges?

A big new market has been created in Europe offering both opportunities and difficulties. Competition is increasing due to globalisation and restructuring.

Part of these changes are the growing opportunities in Eastern Europe, a huge potential market but with significant risks attached. Eastern Europe is very difficult terrain. It cannot be tackled properly by companies not prepared to take an active role. However, I believe that

32

those companies who can prove themselves in Eastern Europe will be able to acquit themselves well anywhere in the world.

The Consequences of Globalisation for Asea Brown Boveri

What have been the consequences of globalisation and increased competition for companies like my own?

Let me give you some details on ABB. For those unfamiliar with ABB, it is one of Europe's largest conglomerates with 220,000 employees. It has a turnover of around US$30 billion and achieves good results.

How did ABB achieve a successful global multinational role?

First, ABB has been successful as a worldwide company by becoming well integrated locally in each country in which it operates. To accomplish this it has decentralised a lot of responsibility and has successfully restructured and reorganised its operations throughout Europe.

In order to be a successful locally and globally as a company you have to have people capable of handling this style of management.

What type of people are needed?

A Euro-manager's profile is complex. It has to combine a lot of things. Naturally the ability to think globally is vital, as is local knowledge and experience. One has to be simultaneously a generalist and a specialist. You need to be able to address very detailed customer's questions and issues, yet you also you need to have a generalist approach.

Flexibility is another key characteristic but you have to combine it with staying power. Finally, you have to be a diplomat and also a leader. So you see that you have to combine a lot of qualities that at first sight which appear contradictory.

The Skills of the Euro-manager

In terms of tasks the Euro-manager has to tackle problems from the top down to the smallest details yet when the problem is solved he is able then to revert and see it again from a high level.

Naturally the Euro-manager has to combine technical competence with managerial competence but beside these multi-dimensional experience is required. That means the manager has to become very familiar with the different environments, cultures and functions of different companies and industries which represents a new challenge. Last but not least it has frequently to be combined with national mobility.

In companies like ABB for example you can expect to change location very frequently. You must also be also fluent in English - not easy for those who are not native speakers. But even more important is that you are able to anticipate the changes which are now taking place in the world.

European Business is Not Developing enough Euro-Managers

We need many European managers armed with such a profile but we have not yet got them. England offers significant possibilities and might prove a most fertile recruiting ground. Countries like German or Switzerland appear is much less promising with the proportion of very senior managers who have international experience being very low.

The shortage also indicates that companies lack an international perspective and strategy in their personnel resource development programmes. In a recent survey when asked about international human resource development programmes, eighty percent of companies surveyed said they did not have one. Without such programmes and policies one cannot expect to develop many Euro-managers except by chance.

Women as Euro-mangers

Where do women fit in to this new breed of European manager? Particularly if they have to change location three or four times in five years, which could be very difficult because of their other responsibilities.

Men and women both possess the qualities required to be Euro-managers, but women will undoubtedly be at a disadvantage if they are less mobile. Mobile women have an equal chance. The main question is not one of gender but rather how quickly we can develop Euro-managers in the requisite numbers.

However, one could ague that more could be done to support women in this area, particularly those with children. Currently ABB makes no distinction between men and women in regard to the level of support given to its aspiring Euro-managers. I also have to say that I do not know of many women who do in fact have children yet are able to pursue a professional career at this level.

Perhaps I should qualify my earlier remarks about high mobility a little.

It is not the norm in ABB that somebody changes their workplace very often, but there are occasions when somebody has to be that mobile, and clearly it is an advantage if they are. If either partner is less mobile due to dual careers they are bound to have to make personal trade-offs between their career and that of their spouse.

Globalisation Needs New Managerial Skills

Summing-up, in response to the new challenges that worldwide companies are facing, especially in Europe, a new breed of managers should be emerging. Unfortunately this is not yet taking place.

The new multinational, or more specifically, European manager needs to have a multi-dimensional profile and to develop this needs global exposure to acquire the relevant experience. In order to achieve this, companies will have to invest heavily to develop the human resources - men and women - to succeed on Europe's new playing field.

PART TWO

The Progress of Equality in Europe

Equal Opportunities:
The Role of the European Commission

Agnes Hubert, Head of the Equal Opportunities Unit, D-G V,
Commission of European Communities, Brussels

Agnes Hubert was appointed to her present position as Head of the Equal Opportunities Unit in Directorate-General Five, based in Brussels, in 1992.

In attending this conference I was delighted to be given the opportunity to address a business-oriented group because the European Commission deals with a variety of issues giving special emphasis to managerial women.

Equal Opportunities in The European Community

As most of you will be aware, the Third Medium-Term Community Action Programme on Equal Opportunities for Women and Men is now in its second year or operation. Three priority courses of action have been selected under this programme : the application and development of the legal framework; the promotion of the occupational integration of women; the improvement of the status of women in society. Significant developments are essential in each of these three fields, if the Community is to witness visible and lasting progress over the next few years. We also need to cement partnerships with all those committed to progress towards sex equality.

I want to touch on two main issues. The first is to tell you about the equal opportunities tools the European Community and member states have been developing. The second is how to use them to recruit and retain more women at managerial level.

The first topic has been well covered by Joanna Foster earlier this afternoon. My thanks to Joanna for having saved me the trouble of going through the arsenal of tools we have got available at Community level. I will concentrate instead on the reasons why Brussels is trying to promote equal opportunities and why we have been trying to make sure that the directives adopted by the Council are properly applied.

In member states you can find a lot of social reasons for promoting women. In the European Community's economy we defend the principle of the free movement of labour, harmonisation of social classes within the Community, and of the defence of competition whilst trying to promote equal opportunity and make sure that all member states and companies can compete on an equal footing.

The second aspect of my speech concerns the use of the Community's equal opportunities tools to recruit and retain women at managerial level.

Making the Working Environment More Attractive to Women

The overall objective for European action is to try and make the work environment more welcoming and attractive to women. I am afraid to say that whichever country you are in - I was very interested in the Norwegian experience - the work environment is not conducive to attracting women. Under the Community's auspices we have been designing some of the essential elements - equal pay, equal treatment, the elimination of inequalities, and equal social benefits - three major areas.

We have also been developing a number of specific tools to try and reinforce the legal framework. We are doing it fairly successfully, aided considerably by the European Parliament and the Council of Equal Opportunities that Joanna Foster chairs and which is composed of many of the member states represented here.

I would also like to stress the importance of the Equal Opportunities Commission in the UK, and the women here who have been reinforcing its message and giving a good example to other European women. A number of legal cases quoted by Joanna were epoch-making in the European Community Equal Opportunities Policy, and they all came from Britain.

That does not mean that equal opportunities are much less in Britain than in other European countries, or to suggest that the actions of the UK's Equal Opportunities Commission action have been much more positive than in other countries.

Diversity Makes Business Sense

Last, but not least, I would like to make two points. One is to get across the message that diversity has a key role to play in organisations. I will use the example of a Danish firm which has a policy that when somebody leaves, for whatever reason, he or she is replaced by somebody of the opposite sex.

We also need to get across a second message that it is better for any organisation to work within a diverse environment. This applies everywhere in Europe. Despite the appointment of a few senior women managers, women cannot play their full role in business until they have achieved a critical mass. Sociologists suggest you need between 15% to 20% of your total management to be women for them to actually play a positive and creative role.

I think these two concepts need greater emphasis within industry. They are not new, but I believe that the Commission's role is to try to be a power in mobilising all the member states to initiate the policies we have got. It is our function to try and find new paths and new ways in which we can move forward.

Better Childcare Facilities
Essential to Irish Women

Mary Wallace TD, Dail Eireann;
Chair, National Womens' Committee, Fianna Fail.

Mary Wallace has been a member of the Irish Parliament (Dail Eireann) since1989 and was a member of the Irish Senate between 1987-89.

She has been a member of the All Party Committee on Womens' Rights since 1987 and Chairs Fianna Fail's National Womens' Committee.

I would like to give an Irish perspective on how government, industry and the European Community can most effectively work together to encourage businesswomen.

This is an issue which has steadily been receiving more attention in Ireland over the past few years. There have been several specific initiatives. I will outline the nature and effect of some of these, and also Ireland's agenda for future action. In addition, I would like to set out how I believe further Community action is essential for equal and effective growth across Europe in developing the contribution of women in the business world.

Women In The Irish Workforce

First, some background on the position of women in the Irish workforce. The most important thing to remember is that the demographic time bomb - so important in other parts of Europe - will not become an issue in Ireland for at least 10-15 years.

Whilst in Ireland, as in the rest of Europe, there has been a dramatic fall in fertility rates, it started later and from a higher base than elsewhere. As such, it is hardly surprising that with a 24% participation rate of married women in the workforce, Ireland lags behind the rest of the European Community. Having said that, the rate is still treble that of twenty years ago. The participation of single women is in line with the rest of the Community. Overall, women currently account for 32% of the workforce, up from 26% twenty years ago.

Encouragingly, most of this growth has come in full-time employment. Further, women in the work force show an increasing level of educational attainment, particularly in terms of third level education. On the negative side, women account for only 14% of the self-employed and are estimated to comprise only 2% of senior managers. This lack of representation at the higher levels of companies is a factor in both Irish-owned and multinational companies based in Ireland.

The Glass Ceiling Operates

Various studies have also confirmed that the problems of vertical and horizontal segregation are just as evident in Ireland as elsewhere. The inequity, and sheer business wastage, of the 'glass ceiling' holding women back has been receiving increasing attention in recent years. In what I believe is a crucial move to dealing with this issue effectively, it has been recognised that you cannot solve the problem solely through action by industry. Action is required on many fronts.

First, and perhaps most important, is the recognition of the importance of education. Considerable efforts have been made in schools to eliminate stereotyping, and encourage girls to choose options on the basis of aptitude rather than gender. This has been accompanied by efforts to promote greater career choices for girls. For instance our Employment Equality Agency has been involved in a project to encourage them to enter the electronics industry at levels other than that as assembly workers or operatives.

More Women With Third Level Qualifications

In third level education an increasing number of females are enroling for vocational courses. For example, women now account for over 40% of those taking business studies at degree level, over double the figure of 10 years ago.

Following education, training has been the next item on the agenda. In this area our National Training and Employment Authority has developed an increasingly successful Positive Action Programme. This programme has worked to encourage women to participate actively in non-traditional sectors, and to develop specific managerial skills.

Women now make up roughly 40% of participants on courses such as treasury marketing and international trade. In addition, there are various women-only courses offered, dealing with areas such as career and skills development. What is particularly encouraging about the Training Authority's programme is that it has also begun to work with employers and employer groups to encourage them to become actively involved in developing women employees.

Encouraging Women Entrepreneurs

In terms of encouraging women entrepreneurs, our Industrial Development Authority has worked to increase greatly the number of women receiving assistance in starting their own businesses. Its 'Women in Business' programme has increased the number of businesses it backs run by women from only 3% in 1984 to 22% in 1989. The programme provided information and advice and actively sought out those women most likely to want to start a business.

These various actions have begun to develop the role of women in all sectors of Irish business. Future progress relies firmly on a continuation of government policy to destroy stereotyping through the education system and on government and business working to extend positive action.

The commitment of government, employers and unions, to action is set out in the current National Programme which runs until 1994. In the programme Government has committed itself to legislative and other action. In addition, The Irish Congress of Trade Unions and the Federation of Irish Employers are working together to guide companies on the implementation of positive action programmes, an approach which, I believe, is vital for steady progress.

Limited Developments In Childcare

In contrast, there has been less concrete progress in the area of child care services. In the European Community, Ireland currently ranks in the bottom four in terms of publicly-funded childcare provision. I hope this will change in the next few years. In the National Programme, government and employers have acknowledged the central importance of the provision of childcare services to achieving real equality in the labour market, and their responsibility for their provision.

Government has begun the expansion of its civil service programme and, in the private sector, the potential for involvement by the European Community through the NOW programme has been recognised, and will hopefully help the expansion of these facilities. This is an example of where the Community is already contributing to womens' participation in business. I believe that its future role will be increasingly vital.

The explicit commitment of the Community through the Social Charter to: 'intensified action to ensure the implementation of the principle of equality' is a step with tremendous potential and one which should be welcomed in every Community country.

Importance Of Protecting Part-time Women Workers

I believe that the major thrust of the implementation of this commitment will rightly come in advancing the rights of that section of the female workforce who are currently most exposed to an internationally competitive situation, which encourages lower and more flexible cost structures. I do not believe that there can be a radical, and lasting, change in the valuing of womens' contribution to business if female work continues to be concentrated in what are frequently, low paid, uncertain and part-time jobs.

More specifically, in the area of encouraging European business-women, the Community's institutions should have an increasingly important role. This very conference is a case in point. With so much activity taking place in the various Member States, the sharing of information is key. I believe it was the former British Health Minister, Aneurin Bevin, who said "Why gaze into the crystal ball when you can read the book?" Through the Community we have an ideal opportunity to concentrate each government's efforts on proven initiatives.

Government's Future Role Is In Education And Training

Overall, in Ireland, while we are not subject to the skill shortages that face other parts of Europe, the imperative for action in advancing the role of women in business has become recognized and there has been some progress. Government has accepted its central role in overcoming traditional cultural barriers, particularly in the field of education and training.

As for the future, Government, Employers and Trade Unions have reached a consensus on what needs to be done in both the public and private sectors. The central importance of child care services to allowing women to continue to use their skills and advance their careers has been accepted and I hope progress will be made.

The role of the Community in raising the status of women in the workforce is, I believe, key. In addition, the Community can work to coordinate and assist the various initiatives of Member States.

Do Danish Women Exclude Themselves from Leadership?

Grethe Fenger Möller, Chair, The Equality Council, Denmark

Grethe Fenger Möller became a Member of Parliament in 1977 and was Minister of Labour in Denmark between 1982-86. She has been a member of the Conservative Party since 1975 and has sat on various committees including Social Affairs.

Grethe Fenger Möller became Chair of the Danish Equality Council in 1987.

Women now constitute 46% of the Danish labour force. The number rose between 1967-1986 from a third to a half - a significant increase. Part-time work involving women also decreased during these years.

Most women now return to work after maternity leave. The availability and high quality of Denmark's public day care facilities enables them to do so.

In common with many other countries, Denmark has had great difficulties in breaking down the traditional sex pattern in education, training and the labour market. As elsewhere, women are very often at the bottom of the hierarchy.

Many women are now financially independent, even though we still have a major difficulty in closing the wage gap between men and women, which remains unsatisfactory.

Few Women In Leadership Positions

We have been studying why there are so few women in leadership positions in the labour market. The influence of gender socialisation, gender specific qualifications, and abilities, have all been important factors in limiting womens' ability to pursue a career and obtain promotion. It was also felt to be important at the organisational level to try to identify the culture of the individual workplace.

The consequences of gender socialisation are apparent in education and career choices, and to the priorities accorded work and family life. Gender stereotyping limits the development possibilities of both sexes, and highlights the maldistribution of power between them.

A sexually divided labour market leads to a lack of women in the education and job categories that leaders are typically recruited from. Women also tend to hold job functions that do not provide the qualifications and experience necessary for management.

However, it is even more difficult to explain why there are so few women leaders even in areas they dominate. One example of this is in schools where men occupy the leadering positions at all levels in both administratiion and teaching. The same inequalities exist in academic jobs in respect of wages, conditions of work, leadership and unemployment.

Because of this we have been studying workplace culture and the opportunities and constraints that men and women experience regarding promotion in different organizations.

Are Women Excluding Themselves From Leadership?

A very important debate in Denmark centres on whether women are deliberately excluded from promotion and leadership, or whether they exclude themselves by not seeking such positions.

In order to find out more we conducted a study which showed that neither having children, nor the nature of men and women's work tasks was responsible for women's limited promotion prospects.

Generally speaking there was no difference between the tasks that men and women did. Also there was no difference between men and women with respect to on-the-job-training, or in attitudes towards working women with children.

Neither could the relatively few women in leadership positions be explained by organisational attitudes towards work, or to the fact that leadership qualifications were defined to a greater extent in accordance with male rather than female ones. However our studies did show that, while some women did want to be leaders, women would often wait to be invited before applying for such positions.

The most important outcome of the survey was convincing many women that having small nunbers of women in leadership positions was due to fact that men choose men. This in turn was either because it was a tradition in the organisation, or because the qualifications linked with leadership positions were either not possessed by women, or that women were simply ignored by men.

Another reason given was that it was a tradition whereby male leaders picked out young, promising men and gave them increasingly demanding and challenging tasks and placed them in higher and higher positions until they ended up in the boss's chair. This seemed to have a great influence in those organisations viewed as male dominant. In this way attitudes, values and rules of behaviour were identified in ways which made the male the norm.

Male Dominant Culture A Powerful Influence

The presence of a male-dominant culture was particularly apparent in appointments to leadership positions. It was less evident in the daily life of the organization. It did not express itself by defining women as different or by emphasizing male characteristics and qualifications as the ones that counted. But it did express itself by underlining the fact that taking responsibility for children and family was incompatible with having a career - a view often shared by the organization as a whole and by the women it employs.

In short, women are allowed to progress in male dominated companies as long as they resemble men, especially with respect to responsibilities outside the workplaces. As long as women have family responsibilities they will have a hard time getting to the top - it is a promotion barrier.

Earlier I mentioned the concept of women excluding themselves from leadership. One can interpret the combination of the exclusion of women, and womens' exclusion of themselves as the result of covert 'negotiations' on the meaning of sex/gender that women and men are always conducting in an organization. Negotiations in this context are to be understood as the daily exchange of points of views, attitudes, values and actions that are part of the definition of reality, and continually adjusted, maintained or renewed. The quotation marks indicate that this does not concern negotiation in the normal sense of the word i.e. planned talks between two or more parties which follow a certain pattern on the basis of a well defined subject, and with the intention of reaching definite conclusions.

Do Women Seek Lower Profile Tasks?

Concerning the distribution of work tasks, both women and men agree that their distribution by sex does not apply to daily activities. It applies first and foremost to those tasks carrying prestige and of primary importance to the leadership. It was a generally held opinion among women that these prestigious tasks were usually offered to the men, and that gender is very important in their allocation.

In this respect womens' understanding was often different from men's. Men did not see the influence of gender in the distribution of the tasks as decisive, but as accidental. In their opinion such allocation was determined by personal preferences, qualities and qualifications, or by timing. That is, being in the right place at the right time. Men held that differences in the workplace were not due to gender but for other reasons. For instance, the difference between the able and the competent employees and the less able and less competent employees. This went for women as well as for men. Or they pointed to the differences between those who have children, and those who do not, men as well as women.

The men underlined that there were women who participated in the prestige tasks, and therefore they argued that the allocation of tasks was not connected with sex/gender differences. The women on the contrary argued that there are very few women who performed these tasks.

In our studies women and men disagreed on whether there was a tendency to exclude women, but they both agreed that there was process whereby women excluded themselves. They agreed that to some extent women avoided the more prestigious tasks because they were interested in different ones - tasks with substance - as they were characterised.

Whereas the prestige tasks have to do with the political system in an organisation. Another way of avoiding involvement with such tasks was by adopting a style of working that was thorough and careful, inimical in some business cultures with performing the prestige tasks, which are more allied to fast responses to management.

Women Lack The Experience Required By Business Leaders

Men excluding women and women excluding themselves must both affect women's promotion possibilities, especially when the distribution of tasks by gender excludes them from the very types of experience traditionally required for leadership positions. Women understand that the qualifications demanded in leadership positions are those possessed by men. The sexual divisions in tasks and ways of working benefit men to the exclusion of women.

Men stressed their relationship with their boss to a greater extent when they described the conditions necessary for promotion. For a man it was important to have a good boss, who could carry him up the hierarchy. It was also important to promote your boss and support him, besides of course being capable and securing the right tasks for oneself to become visible. This concept does not really figure prominently in the female universe.

From a man's point of view it seemed women were excluding themselves - women choose tasks in the organization that may have a high priority but did get the leadership's attention. However, most men choose the prestigious tasks and were very conscious about what they were doing at any given moment. The men choose the tasks out of interest, they also perceived the prestigious tasks as the most exciting ones. From a woman's viewpoint this looks like excluding them.

In my presentation I have tried to give you an idea of what our preliminary studies have shown in the field of workplace culture, and gender differences and their significance for womens' management opportunities. I think it is very important for women to be aware of all the mechanisms I have mentioned. I started by telling you that there are almost as many women as men in the labour force, but women do not work in all jobs, and there are still very few in management.

Liberal Maternity Laws Cost Italian Women their Jobs

Etta Carignani, President,
Italian Employer's Association of Managerial Women

Etta Carignani is co-owner and Managing Director of Weissenfels Steel Industry, the president of a publishing company and co-proprietor of a hotel.

Etta Carignani is also a key member of Femmes Chefs D'Enterprises Mondiales, one of Europe's most powerful womens' networks, and is currently heading an FCEM task force seeking to establish closer links with women in Eastern Europe.

I am joint owner and Managing Director of Wiessenfels, a world leader in the production of chains, where I have special responsibility for foreign sales and developing new markets.

I am also the President of the Friuli-Venezia Guilia Delegation of AIDDA - the Italian branch of Femmes Chefs D'Enterprises Mondiales (FCEM) which has 28,000 members world-wide - and bring you the greetings and best wishes both of Lidia de Uarbeis, our National President and our World President, Maria Grazia Randi. AIDDA represents 1200 women entrepreneurs from the whole of Italy. FCEM is also present in the UK through the British Association of Women Entrepreneurs.

Our organisation has a permanent representative on the National Commission for the achievement of parity between men and women, which answers directly to the Prime Ministerial Office.

The National Commission For Equal Opportunities

The National Commission for Equal Opportunities, presided over by Yina Anselmi, a Member of Parliament, was instituted by the Prime Minister in 1984. Since its inception progress has been hampered by a rapid succession of governments rendering large scale planning impossible.

This situation changed on June 22nd, 1990, when a three year mandate was legally enacted which assures the fulfilment of the precept in Article 4 of the Commission's constitution, namely promoting equality of opportunities between men and women, removing effective inequalities in access to work, removing prejudice in professional advancement, and promoting the integration of women in technologically advanced sectors to enhance the social, political and cultural progress of our country.

The National Commission is made up of twenty-nine women selected as follows:- Eleven are chosen from among the political parties; seven from the most representative womens' associations and movements at a national level, three from the biggest trade union organisations, four from women's entrepreneurial and cooperative organisations at a national level and finally, four women who have distinguished themselves in the scientific, literary and social fields. The choice is made by the Prime Minister himself and enacted through his decree.

The Commission works in collaboration with the departments and offices of the General Secretary of the Prime Minister's Office n Palazzo Chigi, where it has its own office.

All Bills passing through Parliament are studied by the Commission, whose working parties draw up counter-proposals and important modifications. The Commission has succeeded in modifying the Finance Bill, and in passing several innovative laws for women: equal opportunities for women in work, the raising of the age limit in job competitions, incentives for women entrepreneurs and maternity benefit for self-employed and professional women.

To assess the implementation of equal opportunity policies in Italy the Commission has used the results of detailed research, on the activities of the Regional and Provincial authorities, carried out by CENSIS in the autumn of 1991. The survey found 84 Commissions set up by Regional, Provincial and Town Council authorities in Italy, with a total of 1,212 representatives.

Nearly half of these Commissions are in Northern Italy, about a third in Central Italy and slightly more than a fifth are in the South.

The Commissions are a comparatively recent phenomenon with almost 80% set up since 1986. Nearly half of the Regional Commissions were established before 1985 - mostly Regional Womens' Consultative Commissions - whereas Provincial and particularly Town Council Commissions have been slower to develop.

The analysis of representational characteristics has produced a number of disparities, with the cultural world poorly represented and very few ordinary citizens or male executives.

The Role of the National Commission

For the most part the Commission's activities tend towards a cultural and anthropological "mission" aimed at undermining prejudices and stereotypes that produce attitudes, behaviour patterns and acts of discrimination.

Their mainly educational role is reinforced by their main activities - 83% of the Commissions have promoted studies and surveys, and almost 80% have organised seminars and conferences.

The principal problems encountered by the Commissions have led to the depressing conclusion that financial resources and institutional impetus constitute the driving force of an effective development for women.

The First National Conference of Equality Commissions was held in Rome between January 24-26th, 1992. The following three priorities emerged:

— The desirability of a communications network linking the Equality Commissions nation-wide with the National Commission and political institutions, with reference to the European scene, and the new social and cultural factors emerging internationally.

— The need for an increased presence of women in the country's political institutions and in decision-making roles, consistent with their quantitative weight in society, as was reiterated at the round table discussion which concluded the conference. At a time when the traditional forms of political representation in this country are being brought into question - although they are still a guarantee of democracy - it is emerging very clearly that there is a need for the "resource" constituted by women.

— Starting with the forthcoming election, a need for the political parties to encourage the election of women so that the next legislature will be able to introduce the reforms the country expects with their decisive contribution, and so that real democracy can be achieved with a re-balanced representation.

The Influence of European Commission Directives.

I will now turn my attention to the laws and initiatives for the achievement of equality between men and women at work, and the part played by EEC directives in their bringing about transformation.

The principle of equal rights for men and women workers was enshrined in Article 37 of the Italian Constitution in 1946. This principle represented a radical innovation compared with the previous period in which women workers were constitutionally considered as a weak workforce (called a half-force) whose principal need was for protection.

However, implementing this principle has been anything but automatic. It has required a long process marked by several stages, each of which has involved specific issues, strategies and operational solutions.

This process is still far from complete, although its results have become apparent.

The first stage included laws that opened various public careers to women, for example the magistracy and the police. And Law 66, which gave women access to all public offices, and established their right to follow public career structures up to the highest levels from which they had hitherto been excluded, in 1963. It also included a law protecting working mothers, updated in 1971, that forbade the dismissal of women employees from the beginning of pregnancy up to their child's first birthday, and another which forbids the dismissal of women on the grounds of marriage.

The question of equality began to take on a more precise form at the beginning of the 1960s with the establishment of EEC bodies under the Treaty of Rome - Article 119 lays down the principle of equality, although confined to pay. The main result of initiatives adopted in Italy in response to the issues raised at EEC level concerned collective bargaining.

It was not until 1975 that the EEC adopted measures binding on all member states. The first of these was the directive (75/117) on equal pay, which marked the beginning of a period of intense activity in the EEC and its member states, aimed at the formal and substantive acceleration of progress towards equality.

This activity produced two more fundamental directives (76/207) on equal rights for men and women in access to work, professional training, career structures and working conditions and 79/7 on social security. These were followed by the five-year 'Action Plans' which establish the stages of the process of development, and indicate the means and initiatives necessary for their completion, either through binding measures or just guidelines. The Third Action Plan 1991-5 has just been adopted.

The Application of EC Directives in Italy

In Italy the Community directives were adopted in 1977 in a law banning discrimination in access to work, professional training, pay, the assignment of roles and duties and careers. The same law removed some inequalities in social security. It confronted the problem of improving the division of child care responsibilities between parents by allowing working fathers, alternately with working mothers, some of the time-off for child care laid down by the law protecting mothers rights. It also provided a special procedure for dealing rapidly with court cases involving sexual discrimination or political, trade union, racial, linguistic and religious discrimination covered by the worker's statutes.

Legal application has not been entirely satisfactory and it has not substantially changed working conditions for women. It has removed the most direct and blatant forms of discrimination but not indirect and hidden discrimination. Its legal provisions have proved too weak to guarantee women protection in the courts and working women have rarely taken legal action. It has not rectified women's basic inferiority in the job market.

Working Women And Job Opportunities Have Increased

The most substantial change in recent decades - which may be put down to the law on equality, but which has certainly been influenced by other social and economic factors and to the progress of women's emancipation - is the considerable increase in the availability of jobs for women. The number of women in work registered an all-time low of about five million in 1960. By 1987, ten years after the introduction of the law on equality, the number was more than eight million, and in 1990 just under nine.

All young women enter the job market in the same way as their male counterparts. But there are also large numbers of adult women, housewives or women who left their jobs when they married, or had children, returning to the job market. In 1989, 665,000 adult women were looking for work, compared with 231,000 men, the number of young women not working was about the same.

Not all women available for work find jobs, but in statistical terms the increase in working people registered, from the passing of the equal ity law to 1989, was entirely accounted for by women.

There is, however, a big difference in unemployment rates between the two sexes. The figure for men is about 8% while for women it is over 18% - in 1989 in absolute terms there were 1,577,000 women looking for work against 1,153,000 men.

The preference of employers for male workers is particularly evident in cases where they are allowed to offer a position to a named applicant, as with job training contracts. In 1989 the men employed under this type of contract outnumbered women by 60%. This represents an improvement on the previous years since these contracts were introduced in 1980.

On the other hand part-time work, addressed by legislation for the first time in 1984, operates to the clear advantage of women, and has brought about an increase of several hundred thousand people in work. The measure must be considered a favourable one, although a good number of women accept part-time contracts because there is no full-time work available. Though it must also be said that a considerable number of women have also changed to part-time contracts - over 40,000 in 1989, and slightly smaller numbers in the previous years - usually for family reasons.

Significant changes have also come about in the proportions of men and women working in various sectors of economic activity. There has been a considerable increase - including a proportional increase compared to men in the service sector - in women employed in traditional jobs. The same is also true of more avant-garde sectors such as advanced services and the social services. The numbers of women employed in industry and agriculture have fallen - in 1989, out of 100 women in work 67.9 were in the service sector (against 64.1 of men), 23.2 in industry (37.6 men) and 8.8 in agriculture (8.3 men). The corresponding figures for 1980 were 55.7, 28 and 16.3).

Although these trends are generally positive, they cannot obscure the numerous problems that still beset working women, including those specifically related to equality. The stage following the establishment of formal equality is still under way. It aims at the achievement of effective equality and equal access to jobs for men and women in terms of professional training, pay and the assignment of roles and duties in the career structure.

Positive Discrimination Measures Are Being Taken

The problems still remaining to be solved concern the fundamental question of working conditions, and affect the dual responsibility towards their families and jobs faced by an increasing number of married women. Choices of profession are often dictated by tradition, and are not tailored to the real demands of the job market. Basic and professional training, although showing a continuous improvement, must take account of the high levels of qualifications that will be required by the impact of the single market in 1993. Unemployment is still at a very high level - the same applies to the non-employment of women. Womens' work is still the object of prejudice and remains undervalued

In Italy there are many and varied measures being taken to deal with these problems collectively called 'positive measures' or 'positive discrimination'. These are specifically aimed at helping women overcome the obstacles they are faced with at work. Mention should first be made of measures in support of womens' employment and a number of laws governing work - starting with a 1977 law on company conversion and restructuring which states that at the completion of a takeover or restructuring process, the numbers of women employed must not be lower than at the start.

Along the same lines, other provisions concern: reductions in social security contributions for employers who take on new women workers; priority for the approval of subsidised plans aimed at alleviating unemployment (even temporarily) if they predominantly concern women: the introduction of "equality advisors" on Regional and National Employment Commissions which adopt employment programmes, and others besides. The trade unions, in the context of public and private employment contracts, have introduced joint committees with the task of promoting and assessing the achievement of equality in all aspects of work relations.

In local government, particularly at the level of Regional and Town Council authorities, as well as in the Ministries and other public bodies representing women workers and trade unionists have been instituted along the lines of the National Commission for the Achievement of Equality in the Prime Minister's Office, although their responsibilities are different.Their roles involve consultancy in equality with respect to the institutions they work under, the identification and control of discrimination, and the promotion of women in the various field of social life.

Italy's Main Laws In Favour Of Women

I shall now review the main laws passed in recent years in favour of women.

Italy's most recent maternity law is extremely advanced and compulsory. Only Germany's compares with it in terms of generosity. However, the provisions are so generous I think it will rebound on women. I cite as an example one very civilised region of Italy, where young girls looking for a job now have to promise not to marry and have children. This shows how careful one must be in drawing-up legislation. Laws too advanced can have a drastic effect on the employment of women.

The European Community has proposed fourteen weeks maternity leave. Well, Italy now offers two months preceding the delivery date - that can sometimes be extended to three if the women is employed in particularly heavy work - and three months following childbirth. The mother also has a right to absent herself from work for a period of six months during the first year of her child's life. Furthermore, in the case of a child's illness during its first three years she may stop working after presenting a medical certificate.

She also has the right to take either two one hour breaks, or one two hour break every day. Where the working day is less than three hours the permitted break will only be one hour. Furthermore, she may give sixty days termination notice and there are maternity allowances for part-timers until her child's third year.

This law is very progressive from certain points of view but it will severely dent womens' job prospect. Private industry has to pay considerable government taxes to support both it and our health laws - which should be shouldered by the Ministry of Health. It hardly seems fair that private enterprise has to fund all of these compulsory policies.

Another important piece of legislation was enacted on 10th April 1991 containing positive measures for the achievement of equality between men and women in work.

Legislation - Helping Or Hindering Women?

Finally another recent legislative measure favours women in enterprise. It has been approved by both chambers of Parliament, but is still awaiting the signature of the President of the Republic. In order not to take up any more of your time I shall distribute copies of the bill together with an explanatory text.

The coming years will tell whether this, and other laws, are able to make an effective contribution to the solution of at least some of the problems standing in the way of real equality between men and women in work.

To sum up my personal reflections. Italy has the most advanced social law in Europe. Yet it can sometimes be too progressive making it very difficult for women to find a job. The real work is still to expose inequalities.

Norway - A Paradise for Women?

Ase Klundelien, MP, Chair, The Equal Status Council, Norway

Ase Kludelien was elected to the Norwegian parliament in 1989 as a Social Democrat. She was also Norway's first female mayor (Buskerud County) between 1984-87.

Ase Kludelien was elected as Chair of Norway's Equal Status Council in 1989.

People from other countries tend to have a rosy picture of women's status in Norway and in the Nordic countries, feeling that it must be a paradise for women with extensive economic independence, legal protection, social benefits and lots of political influence.

Well it is true that the employment rates and educational level of women in Norway are high; 70% of women are in the labour force; and in the universities female students are in the majority. It is also true that womens' rights are protected by law, that we have quite a well developed social security system and that women's participation in political bodies is high. Indeed, the Norwegian Prime Minister - one of the top seven female political leaders in the world - last year appointed a government consisting of nine women and ten men, the highest number of women ministers anywhere.

Nevertheless, men still hold many of the most powerful positions in Norway, especially in business life where they control most of the economic resources. Masculine values also still dominate our culture. Despite good intentions and nice words about equality, women are still often prevented from fully developing their abilities and ambitions in the labour market.

The Development Of Equal Opportunities In Norway

We still have far to go before having de facto equality between the genders. On the other hand we are aware of (and proud of) what we have achieved - both in a historical perspective and compared to other countries.

In the 1970s we initiated several important social reforms to promote equality. Since 1971, the National Curriculum for schools state that active efforts shall be made to promote equality between the genders. In 1975 we had the Kindergarten Act requiring municipalities to establish and develop nursery schools.

The development of child-care institutions has been going on since then, but it has been a hard and slow process. In 1970 only 3% of children under seven years of age were in day-care centres. And still there is a great gap between the need for child-care and the spaces available. Only 36% of children were in such centres in 1990. Compared to most other European countries this is a low figure.

One of the explanations for this is that Norwegian children start school at seven years of age. Currently there are plans to have compulsory education school start at the age of six.

In 1977, The National Insurance Act was amended, so as to give women eighteen weeks paid maternity leave - previously it was twelve. Gradually, maternity leave has been extended to 2+33 weeks on full pay and 2+42 weeks on 80% pay in 1992.

Norway - A Paradise For Women?

From next year there will be one year of parental leave (80% pay). This will also probably including 6 weeks which have to be taken by the father - the idea being that fathers and children should become closer and that fathers should take their share of the responsibility for their youngest children. Single mothers may take a whole year. Since 1978, the Abortion Act gives the pregnant woman the right to abortion on demand. One of the main arguments for this Act was that rich women could easily go to the UK and have an abortion at private health clinics, whereas poorer women did not have that choice.

In 1979 the Equal Status Act came into force, including an Equal Status Ombud (the first in the world) and an Appeals Board. The purpose of the Act is to prevent discrimination, promote gender equality and was aimed particularly at improving the position of women as they were perceived as being the more discriminated against. This was one of the more controversial features when the Act was passed. Following a lengthy debate, the Norwegian Parliament decided on a wording which was not completely neutral regarding gender. In retrospect, this emphasis has proved to be of the greatest importance in the work of the Ombud. But the wording is still under debate!

The Equal Status Act 21 lays down that there must be 40% representation of each gender in all committees appointed by government or local public authorities. However, the law is not always respected on this point. For elections to Parliament, county councils and municipalities the parties can decide for themselves how they pick their candidates for the ballot lists, but three parties (Labour, Liberals and Socialist Left) have a self-imposed rule that they will have quotas of minimum 40% of each gender on the ballot lists. Norway has proportional representation so each ballot list may get several nominations.

From its inception in 1979, the Equal Status Ombud has received 7260 complaints about violations of the Equal Status Act. (2137 cases have been brought to a conclusion or dropped for other reasons). Discrimination, primarily discrimination against women related to working conditions in both the private and public sectors, constituted 58% of all these cases.

71

During the 1980s it became increasingly obvious that our society was not prepared for the new pattern of dual career families. The organisation and coordination of daily activities results in various forms of time-related stresses and pressures. Women effectively do two jobs, at work and at home. As a result of their greater participation in the workforce, women have increased their total working hours, especially the young mothers who now seem to be working full-time. At the same time, statistics prove that fathers with young children are in the group that does the most overtime. Not only because they need the extra money, but because men normally pursue their career vigorously during the period when their children are little.

The present (Labour) Government has child welfare as one of its three main goals. It has implemented an ambitious programme to improve the situation, for example:

— More child-care centres

— Reforms to deal with the mismatch between working hours for nd school hours, especially for young children

— Radical extension of parental leave

— Special measures for children suffering from neglect or bad treatment

In the equality process, increased and more differentiated education for women has been viewed as one of the key issues in increasing women's influence and power in society and reduce gender segregation in the labour market. The policy for equality during the 1970s and 1980s was aimed at encouraging women to undergo more training and undertake more non-traditional forms of education.

Norway's Gender Segregated Labour Market

Norway has one of the most gender-segregated labour markets in the western world, according to OECD statistics. This segregation has not been much reduced, in spite of extensive campaigns, among them the 'BRYT-project' (Break-project) implemented and run by the Nordic Council in all Nordic countries in the period 1985-89. The results were modest.

Today the Nordic Council is running a new 4-years-project, 'Equal Pay in the Nordic Countries', focusing on wage fixing, legislation, the criteria for job evaluation and methods of compiling applicable data. Women's traditional choice of occupation should be more highly valued, particularly regarding pay. We hope that the project will result in proposals on how to eliminate the barriers which cause pay disparities between women and men. Statistics show that women in the same trades, doing the same type of work, still earn an average of 15 percent less than their male colleagues.

Some gender disparities cannot be explained by differences in age, education, or seniority. Often well entrenched, these discrepancies seem to be very difficult to eliminate.discriminatory job-advertising has been nearly erased but discriminatory practices still exist in recruitment, dismissals, etc.

Positive Discrimination Has Begun

Employer's organisations and trade unions have, to some extent, agreed upon measures for recruitment involving preferential treatment towards the under-represented gender, i.e. women in leading positions and jobs of great responsibility. These agreements now apply generally - in theory - to all state and government agencies and in most municipalities. Such schemes involve so-called 'positive discrimination' to a moderate degree, stating that a woman shall be preferred if she is equally or approximately equally qualified for a position.

Debates about what it means to be 'equally qualified' are ever-present. The public is informed of the special recruitment conditions when the post in question is advertised as vacant. The advertisement then includes the following phrase: 'Women are encouraged to apply'.

This has brought results, but many women who respond to the invitation to apply find that they are not given any favourable treatment. In practice it depends on the person(s) responsible for the appointment

73

whether a moderate amount of positive discrimination is practiced. There is also the option of a complaint to the Equal Status Ombud.

European Community Membership - A Mixed Blessing?

Norwegian authorities are concerned with the problems that young women are leaving the districts, and moving into towns. Measure have been taken to make it more attractive for women to stay in the districts, and to create local employment for them. Courses are available for women who want to start their own enterprises, with grants and favourable loans to small businesses. We are not sure if those measures can be continued if we join the European Community.

Norwegian women hope that the EC will better their situation with equal pay for work of equal value. On the other hand, there is also a fear that a closer connection with the European Community will create a political climate in Norway for lowering its social standards in some fields, and that the competition between the firms in Europe will be so tough that the employers will lower their costs by not fulfilling their social obligations towards their employees.

Today, gender equality has become a commonly accepted ideology in Norway. But some of the changes that have taken place, may easily be reversed if unemployment continues to grow. Ideas of bringing women 'back to the home' remain. Norwegian men and women are hampered by tradition in their views on womens' careers. Women still have the main responsibility for children and household, which hampers many women in their professional career.

There is also the traditional idea that the boss should be a man. This attitude also has an influence on single womens' career opportunities. Such attitudes must be brought into the open, discussed and analysed. Not to give women highly responsible jobs in managerial roles is a waste of talent that a modern society like Norway can ill afford.

own firm. Senior women managers employed in industry are the exception rather than the rule.

By way of illustration: in the Federal Republic of Germany there are approximately 29 million employees and nearly 12 million women employers and employees, of whom 590.000 run their own businesses.

Few Female Managers Among Germany's Technical Professions

Among the most important aims of our Association are the creation of a better framework for all types of professional businesses. We also conduct political and social lobbying to influence decision making in areas such as womens' equality, the organisation of the workplace, working hours and support for new enterprises. And, following German unification, one of our primary tasks is now offering support to women in the new federal states en route to a market economy.

Today I will be talking mainly about female managers in the technical professions - especially female scientists in senior management. I will not be referring to my own company or German business organisations generally since, although individual companies do a lot in this area, there is as yet no national or coordinated approach to our problems.

The unification of the two Germanys brought about some dramatic changes in the employment of women. In the former German Democratic Republic (GDR) 96% of women were employed, a third in engineering. Unification was followed by a dramatic cutbacks in employment - 12.000 women engineers alone lost their jobs.

Despite this the German economy urgently needs qualified women. It is of extreme social and economic importance to improve the situation of women by developing their abilities and enhancing their career prospects. We need to create equal opportunities for both women and men in recognition of the importance of the family.

The Number Of Women Managers Remains Low

Although Germany has a Ministry for Women and female politicians are to be found in other ministries as well, there is still a great need for improvement. A few more figures can verify this. They are very similar to those we heard earlier for other European countries.

Only 2% of women employees are in middle or senior management positions in the private sector - such as director or product manager. In contrast, 8% of men have reached senior positions in their profession. The situation is slightly better at the top levels of the public sector and in parliament where the representation of women reaches around 6%.

The Verband deutscher Unternehmerinnen (The Association of German Women Entrepreneurs) has set a good example because, in its associated firms, over one tenth of positions in the middle, and senior ranks, are occupied by women. A start, but a step in the right direction.

Let me expand a little on our socio-economic and political aims. They include not just the question of equal opportunity, but also how industry can cope with a system of legal protection for women. We feel we must avoid putting in place punitive legislation which ends up being counter-productive, actually excluding women from economic life.

Legislation And Quotas Can Be Double Edged

As we heard this morning from Audi, many of the aims that we are seeking to achieve will not be helped by passing laws - this is particularly so for our small and medium sized companies that remain so important to Germany's and, I suspect, every other European economy. In the former West German federal states, approximately 95% of firms are of medium size and generate over two thirds of total jobs.

With over 80% of women employed in small and medium sized firms it would be disastrous if we underestimated the consequences of exacting legislation in favour of women. A careful assessment of the situation is therefore required. There is no doubt that the German economy needs women and they should be given maximum opportunity to optimise their training and professional advancement, but without destroying their current existence.

In our opinion this cannot be brought about by sweeping legislation or imposing female quotas, as favoured by some of the German political parties and special womens' groups. We feel that by resorting to such positive discrimination methods we would only succeed in undermining the efforts of those women who have and are succeeding on merit, reducing them to the status of token or 'quota' women.

However, neither can we ignore the fact that the number of women with suitable qualifications may be insufficient. But we feel on no account should women be deterred from achieving as high qualifications as possible by introducing a fixed quota system for female employment in industry.

The Cost of Compliance Falls on Small Firms

Germany's vital export sector contains many small firms that are already exposed to fierce national, European and worldwide competition. We would not want to add to this cost base, or hamper their management, by imposing overly-sophisticated systems for the legal protection of female workers.

Let me give you an example. In the past few months in Germany a new regulation for a three year educational leave for mothers has been passed. The idea in itself is good, but it includes a guarantee that, upon completion of their training period, women have the right to have their old position back. This produces severe problems, and additional costs for medium and small firms, since no one can afford to leave a job vacant for this length of time. It is also extremely difficult to dismiss the replacement worker without good reason and totally unreasonable on the person affected. Here we can clearly see the disastrous economic consequences of well-meaning social legislation in favour of women.

Nevertheless, reconciling career and family and having to take maternity leave are important themes. Currently working women must climb a ladder with a few rungs missing that can only be scaled with strength and perseverance. However, more and more women are now succeeding in climbing this ladder, sometimes through self-employment - one in three businesses started today in Germany is founded by a woman.

This is increasingly so in the service industry sector, where the new female graduates from universities and technical colleges with qualifications as mathematicians, scientists and engineers are bringing with them a high standard of achievement, and great managerial potential for the technical professions.

Women With Technical Qualifications Are Increasing

During the past 10 years the numbers of female high school graduates are also growing gradually and in summer 1990, 38% of all students were women. In 1979 there were about 8% female students studying engineering science, and by 1990 the proportion of female students had grown to 12%, and 40% of these intending to become architects. Statistics about women graduates in engineering science correspond with the numbers of female students. In 1977 there were 7% female graduates, and by 1986 these figures had risen to 12%.

In 1987 there were a total of 536,000 female students in German universities of which 13% were studying either mathematics or science and 6 1/2% engineering science. However, not all of the signs are encouraging. Only 1 or 2% of engineers are women, and of these around 11% are employed in the building industry. An even smaller proportion of women are to be found in the areas of machinery and processing techniques. There is still much to do in these fields particularly to make engineering science more attractive to women, and to highlight the good career opportunities such graduates have.

It is also unfortunately the case that, even where women are obtaining the necessary technical qualifications, in many instances private and career aspirations for potential female engineers are incompatible. Of the 100,000 female students who began an engineering or science course in 1987, not all will successfully complete their studies, some will wish to continue with doctorates, and others will give family goals their priority. It will not be until the second half of the 1990's that the remaining students who have completed their studies, will have acquired sufficient professional experience to have reached senior positions in the economy.

This is totally inadequate for the German or any other European economy striving to compete in Europe. We must make even greater efforts to encourage women to pursue occupational training for technical management and then to support them in their careers.

PART THREE

Treating Equality as a Business Issue

Is it a taxi, or more likely an ambulance bringing home the exhausted bread-winner? Is it providing a week's rest-cure at a sunny holiday resort at company expense, so that the children can be reintroduced to their parents? I think not.

I do not think that proliferating the concepts and language of 'family friendly' policies in the context of womens' employment assists either employer nor employee. So I will not be talking about these policies, as such. Instead I will be talking about our 'Employment Support Policies', policies which in ICL are rooted firmly in ensuring that individual employees are provided with the reasonable support they require, to enable them to balance the rights and responsibilities they have, both as employees and family members.

Employee Support Must Be Based On Business Needs

In ICL we are also convinced that all such policies should be based on business need. If we do not have a business, we cannot employ anyone. However, such is the nature of our business that people are integral to our continued success, and hence the business needs to ensure that its employment policies create and support employees in a working environment and relationship with the company, which will enable them and ICL to perform to the maximum of which they are capable.

If the notion of such policies conjures up visions of the 1950s - welfare-style personnel officers going off to visit sick UK employees - I must point out that that was not ICL's approach. Excessive paternalism bordering on 'Big Brother' interference in employees' lives outside work is not what is required. In ICL, line managers are responsible for managing their own people. Employees are treated with respect, and allowed to make their own decisions, based on knowledge of the support the company can, or cannot give them at times of stress in family relationships.

Making It A Business Issue

The policies and practices I will discuss require a company to spend money. They also require fundamental shifts in the way they are planned and implemented to gain acceptance throughout any company that introduces such changes. In the time available I can only cover the general approach, the areas we have targeted for action, and what we have done and continue to do about it.

Simple in concept, difficult in practice sums it up. This is a business issue. To treat it solely as a people issue would miss -- certainly for those of us in the IT Industry - the integral nature of people to our business success. Indeed, only by understanding what is driving our business and how it can affect what happens to our people can we formulate and justify changes to employment policies and practices. Treating it as a business issue also gives you the framework against which to consider what changes you may need to make.

What Business Is ICL In?

So, what business is ICL in? ICL's mission is to become Europe's leading international information technology company by applying world class technology and people to understanding and satisfying our customer's requirements.

ICL is already a leading European based information technology company with some 26,000 employees and operations in over seventy countries. It has a successful strategy of growth through investment in research and development, partnerships and joint ventures. Based on 1990 results the companies now forming the ICL group have combined worldwide revenues of US$4 billion.

A technological leader and supplier of high-quality services, ICL was one of the first companies world-wide to have its entire range of products conforming to open standards. But, spread over seventy countries with different employment legislation covering each one, we had to focus in on those areas where we could make maximum impact.

We choose the UK, where the majority of our employees are based and where the extent of government infrastructure supporting employment is significantly less than many countries, particularly in Europe.

ICL's Business Objective

Information technology (IT) is a high-skilled, labour intensive business. We cannot operate without sufficient of the right people with the necessary skills available when required. ICL, Europe's only profitable European IT Company, is expanding its business and needs to attract the right skills into the Company.

We are profitable because we understand that business growth does not always mean increased recruitment. In time of recession, it means making more with the same, or less and to do that you must be able to retain, motivate and develop the people you already have. The buzzword for the above is 'empowerment' of the individual. The reality is performance and productivity improvement - if you can get it.

If we want to retain skills we need to understand why people resign. ICL has traditionally had lower resignation rates than the industry norms - but we can always do better. So we looked at reasons for unwanted resignations from the company to see if there was anything we could do to reduce them.

Overcoming The Barriers To Empowerment

If we want to empower individuals we have to understand what is holding them back and see what we can do about that. We could have spent a long time analysing data, considering alternatives and coming up with new programmes to effect change. But because we treated it as a business issue we forced ourselves to focus in on a few key areas and try to impact those. The 'bite-size' chunks approach - rather then trying to eat the whole elephant all at once.

From our analysis we could see that two major reasons for people leaving were to do with career opportunities and failure to return after maternity leave. In considering our options for change against the background of the business objective we could see that what we were already doing in ICL's Investing in People Programme (started in 1988 - prior to and with no connection with the government scheme of the same name) would, if continued and extended, address the career development issues identified.

Very briefly, this programme provides managers with a framework of procedures covering objective setting, appraisal, job and personal improvement. Through training and development,reward and recognition strategies and procedures, applied consistently to every single employee

in ICL we have the platform for individual and departmental performance improvement, and career development.

In respect of skills retention we concentrated on:

— Reinforcing the company's commitment to individual career development.

— Policy change in the areas of maternity leave where we
would clearly demonstrate the cost of change and the pay-
back.

ICL is taking on an increasing number of young female professionals wishing to return to work after maternity leave. 'Saving' these skills
is key to our continued success.

ICL's Employee Support Policies

ICL improved its maternity policy in two ways: increasing the
amount of payment - we had paid 90% - to 100%. Second, we increased
the time for which payments were made by introducing a 'returners al-
lowance' - based on maternity pay, payable to those who did return for
the 12 months following the birth. This was seen as a direct contribution
towards enabling returning mothers to defray childcare costs in a manner
suited to their personal circumstances.

Employee surveys in several locations had indicated insufficient
need for on-site creche facilities - so we chose to funnel money direct to
the individual. In addition, we provided for more flexible working hours
for returners where we could satisfy both their own and the business
requirements.

Twenty years ago ICL was also the first company in the UK to
pioneer 'Home working' - as it was then, 'tele-working' as it is often
referred to now. We have no formal company-wide job sharing/part-time
policies but any manager who puts a case together and gains approval
can institute this method of working. In our Internal Staff Training Unit
in Windsor, one manager has devised a departmental workload schedule
which covers her business requirements and provides not only part-time
work for the employees (both male and female), but has evolved to such

an extent that the part-timers have also developed their roles and careers to higher levels in the organisation.

In introducing the option of a career break - applicable to both men and women - ICL recognised that some home situations may demand the employee's permanent attention. With the career break we provided the employee with an option they did not have before.

Monitoring Our Progress

Before I go on to talk about our future plans. I should tell you whether our plans worked. Not least, because I have placed emphasis on the fact that our approach was based on a business investment expected to show a return.

The policies came into force late in 1989. We reviewed their operation in late 1990. Even allowing for the effect of the recession, which was only just beginning to bite in our industry, the rate of return of maternity leavers has more than doubled, and some have chosen to extend their leave through a career break.

The cost of the changes was less than that which we would have had to spend on recruiting and training replacements.

And The Future?

However well, or badly our policy and practices are operating we have a responsibility to monitor and review, to see whether further changes are necessary and can be justified. In ICL we endeavour to keep in touch with our employees perceptions of how they are managed, and where they see the need for improvement. Our annual Employee Opinion Surveys can be relied upon to tell us what our employees think of the Company. In addition we have groups of senior women managers who meet to discuss areas where they can make a more direct contribution to ICL's business, and identify ways in which the Company can help.

We keep in touch with what's happening in our Industry. I am Deputy Chair of the Women into Information Technology Foundation. Through that forum, which includes representatives of all the major IT suppliers and users, we keep in touch with the way our Industry is going.

As part of ICL's business planning cycle, our people strategy and plans are reviewed regularly, to ensure that we will have the right people in the right places at the right time, to ensure the organisation - ICL can achieve its business objectives.

Since you are all intelligent and alert you will have noticed that I have hardly mentioned the words 'family friendly policies'. I hope that I have shown you that by treating the issue as a business issue, and not as a pseudo-sociological trend of the month, we have not only put 'families' into a recognisable relationship with the business, but it has meant we have actually achieved something concrete for the benefit of our employees, our business and hence, of course, our customers.

We are in no doubt that relevant employment support policies feed directly into employee satisfaction, and employee capability which in turn link directly to satisfying our customers requirements. Indeed if we get it right and continue to improve our policies based on sound business principles, we can raise our employees perceptions and satisfaction to even greater positive levels and, dare I say - ultimately raise customer satisfaction to customer delight. After all, that is why we are in business, and how can we remain in business.

Third, once acquired, it is only possible to retain your labour force and maximise its long-term potential by nurturing it.

The current situation is set to become worse. The number of older people in Germany is increasing rapidly. Old Age Pension Assurance is now the subject of a major political debate as is the inauguration of a national old person's nursing insurance.

Against this background the future challenge to German industry is not so much helping women to achieve greater equality but in obtaining and retaining qualified personnel generally.

Although the solution to the labour situation is not exclusively linked to women, nevertheless it is astonishing why so few companies see them as the answer to industry's problem. Put simply, women make up half the population and 55% of the labour force. Unfortunately, over half of this is concentrated in the ten classic 'women's professions' like secretary, nurse, hairdresser, shop assistant or teacher.

Women In Audi

Women constitute 13.5% of Audi's total labour force. Not very high, but greater than any other German car maker. Audi first began to develop it's association with women 15 years ago. We were considered pioneers when we opened our industrial and technical training opportunities to 63 women who commenced apprenticeships as tool lathe operators and machinists. Our early experiences included virtually all the problems encountered today by technically-oriented companies in tapping the potential of women. For this reason I want to take our pilot study as the entry point to my presentation.

In the seventies the number of job applicants to German industry, both male and female, was growing. Industry responded by increasing the number of training places to satisfy the pleas of politicians. However, even at that time, the signs of a significant upheaval were already becoming apparent.

In the face of growing competition from the Far East, Germany's car industry within a high wage economy began to turn away from merely increasing production to the idea of qualitative growth based on higher quality products. However, an industry aiming to produce better products began in turn to place increasing demands on the qualifications and skills of its workforce.

On one hand it was clearly foreseen that the simpler, more repetitive tasks then carried out by unskilled workers would one day be performed by machines - manpower had simply become too expensive. However, the new production facilities that took over these jobs also placed higher demands on the operators.

It soon became obvious that, in addition to the necessary increase in qualification required, the aim of achieving better quality products presupposed a general quality awareness. This prompted Audi to undertake regular studies of the company's requirements for qualified personnel. We wanted to know not only how many jobs would be created or lost, but in order to acquire a better understanding of the need for qualifications we also wanted to ascertain what qualifications these new jobs entailed.

Our personnel planning since has confirmed repeatedly that new jobs arising from the automation process necessitate technical training of an exacting nature. This raised the question back in 1978 as to whether our demand for apprentices could be met over the long term.

A Decline In The Number Of Apprentices

Demographic forecasts suggested a declining number of apprenticeship applications for the industrial and technical trades. At the same time, the greater educational opportunities available from the beginning of the sixties initiated a situation which still persists today. A continual decline in the number of pupils leaving school with lower grade educational qualifications. This was a potentially a serious problem for Audi as traditionally we had recruited about seventy percent of our potential trainees from lower level schools whose educational profile was concentrated more on the acquisition of practical skills and thus tailored to our vocational training openings in the industrial and technical sector.

The share of pupils attending lower level schools has halved from about sixty percent 1960 to thirty percent now. Consequently we opened our industrial and technical training opportunities to girls precisely at a time when the supply of apprentices was falling short of demand and girls in particular were searching for apprenticeship training place.

When we started our pilot scheme in 1978 there was one basic one problem associated with industrial and technical training. The assumption that girls and women were not suited to such activities. So we carried out scientific studies in order to examine this. We discovered that, apart from three shift operations and night work, only about five percent of jobs were not suitable for women. Apart from these, no other real obstacles were found. During and after training, the performance of girls and women was shown to match that of boys and men.

Today, more than ten years after our company first introduced industrial and technical vocational training opportunities for girls we can demonstrate that our initiative has borne fruit. The deployment of women in production and quality assurance has proved very successful and turnover amongst female workers is also lower than men.

Finally, many women show a keen interest in advanced training and have acquired qualification for higher grade activities. Our personnel development activities have enabled us to appoint the first instructresses and master craftswomen in Bavaria drawn from this group. So as you can see the prejudices harboured have not turned out to be correct.

The Future Needs

Our forecasts of the labour market however proved accurate. The situation facing industry and the craft trades has changed dramatically and today many companies are in desperate need of qualified people. When it comes to filling training places young people are calling the tune once again.

Despite the decline in male applicants, industry is still not exploiting the women's potential to the extent it could and the situation is getting worse. Not only is it possible to detect a general fall in the number of apprentices but there also a sharp imbalance between the professions. This is further aggravated by the fact that in Germany over half the female apprenticeship applicants still only apply for ten out of the three hundred and fifty or so trades available to them - and this despite the fact that their favoured professions are often most affected by unemployment or poor income prospects.

Equality Is Gaining Acceptance In Industry

However, some positive trends are emerging. Industry has began to accept the equality of men and women, not least because the state of the job market leaves them no alternative. However, education remains geared towards the more traditional distribution of roles and still has to catch up with modern day requirements. Basically girls still play with dolls and boys with cars. Girls attempting to break out of this role soon become labelled as unconventional, tomboyish, or even 'emancipated'! Changing this situation is not only the responsibility of parents and schools but also with the media as covert educators. These factors seem to the main reasons why girls only choose unconventional professions in exceptional cases despite the wide range of opportunities open to them.

Audi's Strategies Towards Women

So what are Audi's strategies for tapping women's labour potential? We have found that the younger generation is far less prejudiced and that it is quite possible to interest girls in training for a technical profession. Although this does necessitate a certain amount of information and communication work. This activity is greatly assisted by the quarter share female apprentices hold in our industrial and technical sector.

To support their careers advisory role we invite schools from our catchment areas to take part in conducted tours of AUDI. Here female pupils are introduced to the vocational opportunities we offer wherever possible by female apprentices who have attended the same school. This relaxed atmosphere promotes a lively exchange of information. Audi also informs teachers of special events staged by the school industry working group, as well as practical vocational training forces put on for secondary school teachers. As you can imagine, the teaching staff at schools frequently provide undecided pupils with important tips and advice.

Last but not least our regular in-house information draws attention to the fact that all professions are also open to girls. This shows our employees, whose children often form a follow-on generation of recruits, the opportunities available to their daughters.

Admission to employee status also forms an important element in the measures we implement to promote opportunities for women. For, as long as skilled female workers are not commonplace on the industrial and technical job market and as long as they have a poor chance being placed in employment, it is only reasonable to encourage a girl to learn a profession of this type if the company in principle is prepared and likely to engage her services after training. By so doing we have gained a measure of credibility and eased the decision making process for many girls - although we do not give them any guarantee of a job.

Irrespective of school leaving qualifications and their sex I feel that all of our apprentices enjoy a high level of training. This training safeguards the occupational future of our male and female employees. However, it is no longer possible for anyone to simply attain a skilled worker's certificate. Such a minimal qualification can be almost as detrimental as not having one, or having the wrong qualification. And it is often the reason for missing the boat half way through one's working life. Audi expects all it's employees to be willing to continue learning after completing their apprenticeship. This applies to both men and women. Based purely on performance, our system of further training provides everyone with equal opportunities.

A greater imbalance exists between the sexes in our skilled and executive personnel. In our company these higher paid positions are usually held by technical college and university graduates. But technically-oriented companies will in future increasingly be forced plug any resources gaps in these two areas with women. The Swiss-based Prognosis AG has forecast a shortage of half a million people with managerial skills in German-speaking companies during this decade. Particularly hard hit will be those industries which are already forced to forgo the services of women because they do not choose to study technical subjects in the main.

At Audi around four fifths of our skilled and executive functions are based around activities of a technical nature. The problems here are similar to those in the industrial and technical apprenticeship trades. Many girls choosing to study engineering feel out of place in lecture theatres mainly populated by male fellow students. The trends suggest that girls still prefer to study social science, medicine or business studies. Only a couple of years ago the share of women among applicants for places at institutions of technical and education was less than three percent.

Due to the shortage of female applicants it is therefore not surprising that men have usually been employed to fill skilled and executive positions. And, in view of their above mentioned study preferences, it is not surprising either that the three female department heads amongst Audi's total of 300 executives all work in the personnel department

Attaining A Critical Mass

But thing are starting to move. More and more women engineers are knocking on our door. Their share of applications has more than double within a very short space of time. Overall our share of female graduates is also showing an upward trend. Although, compared to our total of eighteen hundred graduates, the hundred or so women still appears meagre.

This problem is being tackled in a similar way to that adopted for training in the industrial and technical trades. For some years now being carrying a publicity and advertising campaign on as broad a front as possible. Headlines like 'Who says men make the best managers' have been targeted at overcoming the scepticism with which many women view the technical professions despite their attractive career development opportunities.

However it is not sufficient simply to direct women's interest towards technical studies. They must be directed into the right courses of technical study. It would not be very helpful to us if, for example, architecture and interior design were to remain the favourite subjects for future female engineers. At exhibitions and shows we try not only to present our products but we also try to demonstrate to both male and female visitors the merits of the job opportunities we offer to our skilled and executive personnel.

Our programme for developing individual potential is based on a set of personnel programmes intended to help recognise and foster qualified junior staff development into specialised executives functions. These are also particularly suited to uncovering women with management potential. I also hold regular talks and meetings withe external personnel consultants on promoting opportunities for women.

Against Positive Discrimination

Let's just recap on what I have said so far. I have acknowledged that Audi does not have a detailed strategy to promote opportunities for women in the jobs and apprenticeships we offer. Other companies will no doubt appear far more progressive to you in the level of support they offer women through quotas and the like. However, at Audi we are simply trying to achieve something which should be quite natural - providing equal opportunities and inviting women to make use of them. I am firmly convinced that in the long run our approach is better. To do anything more proactive - using quotas or women's representatives - would engender mistrust in the opposite sex. This is not the case at Audi but this may also be due to the fact that we only employ six thousand women so far compared with about fifty-two thousand men.

However I feel the real reason lies in the fact that we have not approached the subject by imposing top-down directives but by activating grass roots support which achieves greater credibility. Men are not then suspicious of being cheated by women just because a quota has to be filled or because a woman has to be found.

Promoting Opportunities

The third aspect of my presentation is less concerned with equal opportunities and more with their promotion. Here the emphasis is more on the family than women per se. We believe that a harmonious private life is far more conducive to good performance at work than the working environment. We aim our measures at both mothers and fathers, although in practice it is mainly women who make use of them. Here I am particularly referring to Audi's offers of part-time employment and the promise of reinstatement after the birth of a child. We recognise that careful organisation of working time is central to the need to combine family and work.

Over one thousand members of our workforce, i.e. about 3% of the total, make use of our facility to work part-time. Compared with other car manufacturers this represents a very high percentage. In addition to many variants on full time employment we also offer a large range of part-time employment opportunities. We always make an effort to meet the individual wishes of our employees and insofar as operational requirements will permit it. Our part-time package of working four or five hours during the morning while the children are at school remains the most popular. We also have some constraints - female workers may have to work every day on alternate weeks or for ten straight days at the end of the month to help us meet accounting requirements and then take the rest of the month off.

We now offer a total of over 50 part-time employment variations In addition to operational and organisational aspects we also make sure that, in the interests of our female employees that the amount of part-time employment they do reaches a level which guarantees social insurance cover. Also, introducing an hourly work account helps to insure a uniform monthly payment - even in the event of irregular working hours - and in practice there are virtually no limits to shaping part-time employment packages.

Retraining Helps Re-entry To The Workforce

However working part-time is not always the wish of a child-bearing mother or father. Often the mother or father wishes to devote their whole attention to bring up a child during the important initial years of it's life. Audi's response - commencing in 1986 - was to offer the possibility of reinstatement after completion of child-rearing leave. In addition to the social and political aspect of giving mothers and fathers the opportunity to assume their profession after a prolonged break from work to rear children, this strategy was also based on well founded economic considerations

In view of our continuously growing skilled labour shortage our aim was to retain the investment we have made in human capital and bind

112

employees to the company in the long-term. Other companies have since followed suit and but usually their reinstatement offer is contingent upon job vacancies at the time whereas Audi's is virtually unconditional. We have attached one or two caveats to our pledge that various publications have found restrictive. For instance we require that those concerned take part in further training during their leave of absence but we do not consider this so much as a restriction as facilitating their return to working life.

Results of additional studies published from time to time reinforce the difficulties of returning to working life, particularly the problems associated with technical reintegration. To those burdened both with managing a household and maintaining contact with a technically based profession it naturally presents a considerable problem. A lack of family support is the most frequent complaint. However, comparable difficulties are also presented by the need to gain higher job qualifications as the changes of job contents, machinery and equipment.

As such, obliging people to undergo further training during the period of child rearing has been enthusiastically received, as has giving them the option to stand-in for colleagues when there are off sick or on vacation. This contributes towards preserving and brushing up know how. Incidentally, anyone making use of the reinstatement pledge need not fear any loss of seniority or any cut in the social welfare benefits provided by the company. The latter is particularly important in terms of the company pension. Another example is low interest loans granted to employees also continue during the leave period.

At the instigation of our board of directors, a project team entitled 'promoting the vocational opportunities of women in Audi' was set up in 1988 in order to consistently follow up current measures and generate further ideas. One idea of this project team was to instigate voluntary networks for women with common professional interests. We are pleased to say that this idea has met with an extremely positive response. The women involved in the networks provide each other with mutual support and enhance the work of the project team through their ideas and advice.

In addition to effective publicity measures outlined above, Audi also support various initiatives to promote opportunities for women through its involvement and participation in events encouraging exchanges of experience and discussion, as well as by providing financial assistance.

There is one example I would like to make particular reference to - our supra-regional initiative 'deeds not words'. This politically neutral institution encourages management and personnel departments to make greater allowances to qualified female employees within the general personnel policies.

Its main objectives include: opening up fields of activity primarily dominated by men and selectively training women with a view towards their taking over responsible functions in companies. Also undertaking intensive and continual publicity to create awareness with regard to the participation of men and women in industry. As well as promoting jobs and employment flexibility that take into account the requirements of women in everyday life. So as you can see these objectives fully correspond to the aims set by Audi.

We are convinced that we will be able to achieve our goals more readily if the promotion of vocational opportunities for women is supported by a significantly larger number of companies and by society in general.

What Are The Major Obstacles Outside The Company?

In the near future we believe that greater importance should be attached to uniting family and work. In doing so, politicians and public institutions in particular are called upon to make an appropriate contribution and create the necessary framework to give women the assurance that their children are in good hands while they themselves are at work. The public sector should not undermine our efforts for example by stipulating inflexible opening hours for creches and schools because they adhere to the old adage that a mother's place is in the home.

To summarise, let us look at the situation currently prevailing on the German job market. The increasing number of qualified women, the demands for qualified employees in industry and the debate on the qual-

114

·ity of opportunities for women will all help to get things moving. However, changes like this cannot take place without a continual awareness and changes of attitude from all sections of society.

We believe that there are a number of ways to facilitate this process. We in industry must make use of these tools voluntarily before the legislators start imposing regulations which not every company will able to survive and which I believe will generate a backlash against women. Equality is not just a problem facing industry but more fundamentally our society. We therefore need a national social policy geared towards eliminating the division of labour, roles and hierarchies based on gender.

We can all contribute towards greater awareness and ending discrimination against women. This conference is just such a contribution. Events like this can call widely for equal opportunities for women. But they need not only admonish. Here everybody can get new ideas on realising equality for men and women.

I would like to share one final thought with the ladies in the room. To get a chance you have to be better than men and you have to work harder. The observation I offer, based on personal experience, is that's not very difficult!

Demographic Change makes Equality a Strategic Issue for TSB

Fiona Cannon,
Group Equal Opportunities Manager, TSB Group plc

Fiona Cannon was appointed to her present position in the TSB Group in 1992, following a period as Equal Opportunities Manager within TSB Bank.

Prior to joining TSB, Fiona Cannon worked in the Pepperell Unit of the Industrial Society, one of the country's largest training organisations.

The TSB Group has approximately 40,000 employees spread over 3 divisions:

— Retail Banking and Insurance, employing about 30,000

— Commercial Division, which includes Swan National, Wescol, and Property Services

— Hill Samuel group of companies

116

TSB and Equal Opportunities

There are several reasons TSB took action on equal opportunities. Firstly, over the next few years there will be a 41% decline in the number of school leavers. Since 85% of TSB's recruits have traditionally been school leavers clearly we need to begin recruiting from a broader labour pool.

The latest Department of Employment figures also suggest an increase in the numbers of sixteen year-olds staying on in further education which will reduce the pool still further.

In addition, we recognise that we have ignored important sections of the community in our recruitment - sections we now need to tap into if we are to succeed in recruiting the staff with the skills and abilities we need in the 1990s.

Secondly, it costs TSB £7,000 to recruit and train a junior member of staff. The annual cost of replacing those who do not currently return from maternity leave is £3 million. Faced by such costs and a tight labour market, we obviously need to develop the potential of all our existing staff.

Thirdly, the financial sector is becoming more sales oriented. TSB now has different skill requirements. We believe that women returning to work might possess the skills we are looking for, i.e. personal authority and experience.

Finally, we saw that women have not previously developed at the same rate as their male counterparts within TSB. Barriers existed between senior clerical and junior management positions. We recognise that we cannot continue to waste the talent of women within the organisation.

The lowering of the trade barriers at the end of the year will also mean that people will be able to move freely around Europe to find work. We want to ensure that we are an attractive organisation to women who might otherwise seek employment elsewhere in Europe.

TSB's Strategic Approach

Equal opportunities was treated like any other business issue. The key components were:

Top level commitment: with all chief executives, and senior directors have attended a day and a half workshop on equal opportunities. At the very first workshop we held, it was decided that equal opportunities was of strategic importance to the business. It was to be treated like any other business issue. It was decided that each company within the Group would produce action plans for implementing the company policy. These plans would cover every aspect of employment: from recruitment and selection through promotion, training, terms and conditions, as well as customer service.

Managerial accountability: managers are held accountable for implementing these action plans and achieving the results. Each company has to set itself estimates for the composition of the workforce by race, sex and disability which will be the outcome they expect as a result of their action plans. While I am concentrating on women here, our equal opportunities programme covers race, sex and disability. It does not focus on any one group to the exclusion of another.

Training and promotion: training will be cascaded through the organisation with the policy being sold by tying it to business objectives.

TSB has taken a package approach which involves looking at the whole organisation. Without this, I doubt that any of our individual initiatives would work. The key areas were:

— Selection methods must be objective to ensure that talented staff are recruited to the organisation. We are asking our recruiters to be a lot more sophisticated than they have had to be in the past, where they have had a fairly homogeneous group of young applicants. We are asking them to deal with a heterogeneous group in terms of race, sex, disability and age. That means people with different combinations of academic, life and work experiences. Selection methods need to be able to cater for that diversity.

- We need to ensure that women get a fair chance at training and promotion once they have joined the organisation. Otherwise they will not stay and our investment will be wasted.

The objective was to retain staff who would otherwise have left because of domestic responsibilities. We also wanted to recruit high calibre staff from a variety of labour markets by demonstrating a positive attitude to the need to combine domestic and professional responsibilities

TSB's Specific Initiatives

Family Friendly policies came into effect in August 1991. They extended the same rights to adoptive parents as to natural parents and recognised that fathers as well as mothers may wish to take responsibility for the care of their children. Among the key features were the following:

- The period of parental leave after the birth/adoption of a child was extended from 29 to 52 weeks. Those on parental leaver remain TSB employees. At the end of parental leave, staff have the right to return to the same or an equivalent job on the same terms and conditions.

- A maximum of an additional six weeks paid leave is granted to staff who return to work within a year. This payment is in addition to any statutory maternity pay and applies to full-time and part-time staff who meet the service requirements for maternity leave.

- The payment of bonuses e.g. Christmas Bonus and Profit Sharing whilst staff are on parental leave. Previously, no payments for Christmas Bonus or profit-sharing were made until six months after the member of staff had returned to work.

— The reduction in the qualifying requirement from 3 years to 2 years and the extension of the scheme to include care of elderly, sick or disabled dependants. Staff now have the opportunity to take a complete break of up to five years over a maximum of three breaks if required. In addition, all pensionable service prior to the career break is maintained and linked with service from the date of return.

Employers also need to consider the image they portray to potential applicants. We decided to change our advertising image in order to attract more women returners. We want to present a positive image of the range of applicants that we wish to attract rather than simply saying that we are an equal opportunities employer. We want to say that we recognise that talent and skills exist in all sections of the community. The new advertising campaign is not a 'women returners' campaign - it is rather a campaign to attract people from all sections of the community. The images we present include white people, ethnic minorities, young women, older women returning to work after having children, disabled people, as well as our traditional applicants.

A Workforce That Reflects Society

We have made progress from our 1989 figures of women in management. Our long term aim is that the composition of our workforce will eventually reflect more nearly the community in which we work. This will mean approximately 50% women at all levels of the organisation. We believe it will take us a generation to reach this point and I feel the approach I have outlined will assist us in this endeavour.

PART FOUR

Managing the Change

Developing a Strategy
to Manage a Diverse Workforce

Malcolm Greenslade, Group Employment Policy Director,
Grand Metropolitan plc

Malcolm Greenslade joined Grand Metropolitan in 1983 in their Watney Mann and Truman Brewers Company.

A physicist by training, Malcolm Greenslade was Compensation and Benefits Director and VicePresident, Human Resources for Intercontinental Hotels, prior to becoming Grand Metropolitan's Group Employment Policy Director.

I am very conscious that when you come to these sessions and you listen to other people, there are not actually too many pearls left in the mud to discover. What you are actually going to hear are some similarities and, I hope, some differences to what has gone before.

I am going to talk about how Grand Metropolitan initiated and is implementing a strategy for understanding and managing diversity, one of the main objectives of this conference.

Grand Metropolitan is the tenth largest company in the UK, and the largest drinks company in the world with brands such as Smirnoff, Baileys, J & B, Malibu and Cinzano.

In Burger King it has the second largest fast food company in the world after McDonalds, plus other well known brands such as Häagen Dazs, Green Giant, Chef & Brewer Pubs, Express Dairies and, until recently, Peter Dominic. We are very much about being close to customers and consumers. We employ about 130,000 people world-wide, of whom about half are part-time.

It was the acquisition in the USA two years ago of a company called Pillsbury, bringing with it Burger King, that really raised our Group's awareness of equal opportunities issues or 'managing diversity' as it has become better known in the USA. It forced us to take a more global view of equal opportunities and particularly how it was going to affect us in Europe.

What we then had to do, very simply, was secure the attention and commitment of our Board to undertake an initiative in this area.

Securing Board Commitment

The only way that you get the attention of our Board is to be able to show clear business needs around this issue. We are not just talking about the Executive Board. We also had to put our non-executives - people like Dick Giordano and John Harvey-Jones - through the programme as well.

I made a Board presentation to try to identify the very significant business issues that faced us - I am sure they are very familiar to you - based very much on the changing nature of our customers and consumer mix.

We have very high numbers of ethnic minority and female purchasers of our products. As an example of where we were going wrong I took the case of one of our pet food companies in the US . It found from examining its market that there were few minority purchasers of its dog food in high minority areas like East Chicago and Detroit.

The first assumption, that minorities did not keep pets and therefore do not buy pet food, was clearly dispelled by a little research. We then went to ask the minorities why they didn't buy our products. They answered very simply: "look at your dog food advertisements. They comprise white, blond haired little boys and girls, and golden labradors, and don't actually reach out to us or attract us."

The make-up of the pet food company's management was also a significant factor. Based in Pennsylvania, it reflected its mainly white, male population. There was nobody from a minority group in that workforce that could actually say "these are the issues out there".

Managing Diversity In Its Fullest Sense

I was talking to the Board primarily about developing a people strategy that focused not only on women and minorities but on managing diversity in its fullest sense. I think it was a statement by our Chief Operating Officer made that drew together the internal and external dimensions of the problem. "We will become more competitive by reflecting in our employed population the same diversity that exists in our marketplace. Cultural diversity will make us stronger, more flexible and more responsive to business opportunities."

The second thrust was clearly recruiting the best and the influence of the demographic situation. It's easy for us all to talk about demographics but have you actually analysed what it means to your business over the next ten years? In the USA over the next ten years we will recruit five million people. It was not that we had five million jobs, but that the turnover in places like Burger King and Haagen Daas is something like 250% per annum!

People may react to that and say it is appalling. Unfortunately that is one of common threads in similar businesses. McDonalds has it as well. This means, if the level of turnover does not come down, that we are going to have many people going through our organisation and we want to get the best. When you also consider that half Burger King's employees are under twenty-one you can see that the declining availability of young people is an issue that faces us quite dramatically.

Gender, Ethnic And Age Mix

We successfully showed to the Board that in these major areas of employment there were significant issues for us in the future. We were going to have to address the questions of gender, ethnic and age mix.

In the two European countries where we principally operate, the UK and Germany, the problems were more pronounced in terms of more women entering the marketplace, and not so much the ethnic concern that exists in the US.

The third one major issue we presented to the Board was how to get the best out of the people we had already. Here we had to confront the Board with some fairly uncomfortable statistics. Until last year we actually did not know how many women we employed in the organisation. So we established some benchmarks.

We found that among a company that operates in 32 countries 44% of our world-wide workforce were female, with 16% coming from minorities. That was our first baseline. Of course it varied according to the country we were operating taking a Grand Metropolitan perspective.

When we analysed our top 750 jobs we found only 8% female and 1% minorities. Clearly we were not developing everybody's potential internally.

The last point concerned legal requirements. We pointed out that around the world, legislation is changing - e.g., Civil Rights bills in the USA, European Community Directives, etc. Clearly we have a company value and philosophy that says we observe legislation wherever we operate.

But that was not the reason for our needing to take an initiative in this direction. I think we were successful in showing to the Board that there were clear business reasons why we had to have some initiatives. Not just UK initiatives but a global initiative since, although priorities and the strength of the problem changed according to where we operated, it was a universal issue.

Grand Metropolitan's Vision

Following the Board presentation, the first question was "where do we wish to be as a company, what is our vision, what is it we want to move towards?"

In our vision statement we talked about disadvantaged groups and employment. We believed that on our evidence women were a disadvantaged employment group wherever we operated around the world.

A second point that we were very keen to stress was that there is individual as well as managerial responsibility in understanding and valuing the differences between people.

From the vision statement, we wrote a policy. Now, we had had an equal opportunities policy for several years. We produced it when our PR people said "What's our policy?" We never really did anything about it. In saying this I do not think we were a lot different from many other companies, the difference was that now we wanted to do something about it. However, we recognised very quickly that our policy did not differentiate us from any other company. What does differentiate you, are the actions you commit to to put it in place.

Therefore we identified a whole range of activities where we required initiatives, and what we tried to do was to bring about an enduring cultural change everywhere we operated and throughout our activities.

The Importance Of Education And Training

For us, it was not just about equal opportunities in terms of getting the numbers right - and I will come back to this. What do I mean by that? First, that we had to very clearly identify executive responsibility wherever we operated for implementation of the programme. Second, we had to have a very high investment in education and training as our experience in the USA told us these were the most powerful tools for changing behaviour.

We have probably set ourselves a limited objective that you may challenge, but our education and training is designed to change behaviour, not primarily attitudes. We believe that a change in attitude follows from a change in behaviour. That is the direction of our education and training.

We clearly need to establish much more sophisticated monitoring in several areas that does not yet exist around the world. We wish to set and have set improvement goals, not only for the amount of training but also in other areas that we are turning our attention to, such as incentives.

What I mean by that is we have made this a business initiative consistent with the way we manage our business. As it is a business priority, people are rewarded or punished based on their performance in this area. We are looking at the relationship between our suppliers, our franchisees and ourselves and we are specifically looking to increase our supplier base in terms of, for example, minority suppliers and companies that predominantly employ women. Looking also at where we place our sponsorship, the extent to which we can sponsor activities related to minorities, womens' activities, networks etc.

New Policies And Initiatives Were Developed

We are turning attention to advertising and I will come back to it as a big issue. We are looking at sexual harassment. We have one sexual harassment policy across the US and are now looking at how we move it into France, Germany, UK etc.

We have had family responsibility policies for a couple of years including extended career breaks for maternity, extended career breaks for looking after family situations, carers etc. We are at the point of reviewing that now because our experience has shown most our returners do not want three year career breaks.

More important for example is greater flexibility upon return to work, where I think we have missed out and need to rethink. We have some flexible working but we need to make it a lot easier. We are prioritising people with disabilities whom I think are marginalised in this sort of programme. We are looking at special events that we can take part in and promote our commitment to diversity.

Lastly, and most importantly, you need to look at how you communicate your philosophy and values, both externally and internally.

The Process Of Securing Board Commitment

To make it happen in these areas, I do not think you can begin without getting top management commitment. You can, but I suggest that is where you will have the problems, for example when the money gets tight - when it gets taken away from you. Making a business case secures the commitment and agreement to a corporate initiative. However, as in all these cases, a Board can commit to an initiative but not see it through in terms of delegated responsibility. For us that was not sufficient.

The Grand Metropolitan Board had to go through a 24 hour residential programme that brought them face to face with their prejudices and their stereotyping. They also had to set out the Group responsibilities in the business to move it down through the organisation and education and training were the most powerful ways to do that.

I remember sitting at the Board presentation and listening to nine white British males talking about women's issues and about half way through the discussion somebody actually said "How the hell can we talk about women's issues?" So I do not know how other people have done it. We found it particularly important during that workshop that these individuals experienced real situations that they would not actually confront in their normal life. So we selectively introduced a senior woman with a disability, some senior women from minority backgrounds and some successful business women etc.

We made them feel uncomfortable and that was probably the first time I think they had actually come face to face with some of the issues. I can remember one emerging at lunchtime and saying "I think we are on the road to Damascus." The point was that they had to experience it. We used an external consultant to do that although we had great difficulty in selecting someone who could talk with a senior executive team about the issues of disability, gender, ethnic minorities.

Top Down Training

As far as the training was concerned it was to be top down. Again, one thing that we learnt from the US was that if you drive something top down, you usually get a groundswell at the bottom from people asking "What's in it for me? It's going to take a year to reach me but I'm interested now."

So what we are experimenting with is giving seminars to people at the other end of the organisation, which they can attend on a voluntary basis and that start to acquaint them with the issue. Our strategic idea is the training is top-down but that education is bottom up. We are not trying to train people in our organisation in the management issues, we just

129

want to sensitise and make them aware at this point. I have talked about measuring progress. Clearly with the numbers of people in our organisation it is important we measure our progress in terms of training.

Developing Targets And Monitoring

We are also committed to Opportunity 2000. We have not set ourselves specific targets because at this point we have not analysed our businesses over the next three years sufficiently to know what we are capable of achieving. We need, for example, to look at our succession cover and see what's coming through. We would be foolish to set targets that we cannot achieve.

We are establishing something called a 'Diversity Council' composed of senior members from all our businesses who will measure our progress and report twice yearly to the Board.

I talked about accountability. It is an integral part of our business issues, therefore every company has to have a business strategy and plan to address diversity in the areas I indicated. Our top 250 managers all have to have a diversity goal incorporated in their goals that are bonused. We are not actually insisting anybody has a goal until they have been through an education training programme and they understand the need for them to have a personal business objective and to be rewarded based upon it. However the Board came out from the workshop and voluntarily set their own objectives and bonuses straight away.

A Phased Programme

Phase 1 in our education and training programme is to increase knowledge, to increase an awareness of the value of differences that people bring to the workplace and provide people with the skills to manage it. It's a high investment in education and training and I think that's the problem, when times get hard it gets cut.

Phase 2, increasing sensitivity, establishing accountability for goals, building a critical mass of people of colour and women in high positions. We do have a positive action programme to do that. e are taking a twofold approach. The long-term one including recruitment of graduates, putting in development programmes such as 'Springboard' and 'Family Responsibilities' will bear fruit in five and ten years time at senior level.

We are not prepared to wait that long. So for example, whenever we go outside to recruit every headhunter is required to include one female candidate in that shortlist and desirably one person of colour and one person with disability. The reason I say "desirable" is that in reality if people are not there at the higher levels you can only say that is a desirable goal for us to have at least one on the short list. Creating and enhancing a high quality people system has also been built into our appraisal system and potential succession cover.

Matching Culture And Commitment

I want to finish on one area that is perhaps a bit closer to home. It is not just about how you increase or balance the number of people in your organisation. It is how your organisation culture reflects the commitment to it and the way in which you portray yourself to your customers and your employees.

Simultaneously as I wrote our new policy statement following the Board presentation, one of our subsidiaries produced an advertisement that you may well recognise. It came from Häagen Dazs ice cream and caused considerable discussion both externally and internally in the company from both males and females. No real trend emerged, several males and females said "I don't actually find this consistent with one of the values you are trying to establish"; and others said "this is actually good advertising." The debate is: is it sexist, exploitive of women, or merely sensual? The Advertising Standards Authority had 50 complaints and didn't uphold one.

What do we then find?

This same advertisement is now appearing in the papers. Not placed by us but this time by the Newspapers Publishers Association - as an example of very successful advertising! Brand awareness went up from 9% to 16% and sales trebled in the period of advertising. All I am saying is, you judge whether you feel it is right, wrong or consistent. The point is that once you start to go higher profile in your organisation with your employees, do not be surprised if people start raising these issues.

131

I am sure many of your will recognise this. If you are in step it's not such a problem. One of our goals is that our advertising should reflect commitment. Any business that you are in should emphasise that commitment.

Another advertisement placed in the US was a good example of combining product and recruitment advertising. It actually talked about the sort of company that we were, that we were committed to diversity and the sort of people we were looking for.

I would like to finish with a couple of anecdotes. As I said one other area we are looking at is trying to increase our supplier base in terms of investing money in minority groups and communities and businesses with female owners. We did that in the US and were surprised in just one year how many wives of directors joined the boards of supplier companies.

The other one was our annual report where it was pointed out that every female was portrayed in a very stereotyped way, either shopping or waitressing. So it reaches into everything you do, it is not just about numbers.

It is very early days for us, we are going to make many mistakes I am sure, but my point is we have begun to identify some of the issues and act upon them in a strategic manner.

"We Only Discriminate On Ability":

Shaun Pantling, Director of Customer Services Division

Shaun Pantling joined Rank Xerox UK Ltd in 1974, being appointed as National Distribution Manager in 1985. He joined the Board in 1988 as Director of Customer Services and is now responsible for the service and logistics operation.

Shaun Pantling was the sponsor of Rank Xerox's initiative to gain BS 5750 qualification.

I want to talk about the development of Rank Xerox's Equal Opportunities Strategy, including our women in management programme. More specifically, about the process of cultural change that we put in place to bring this about.

I will tell you something about the Company, and for those familiar with Rank Xerox you will know that we never miss an opportunity to sell! Well, this morning I want to sell our organisation, and the real progress we have made towards involving more and greater participation in equal opportunities and in encouraging more women into management.

I will also be talking to you about our culture, because in Rank

Xerox we believe our culture is quite unique. Historically, Rank Xerox has been labelled as white, male, young and boisterous. I'd like to share with you the ways in which we are changing and some values that we believe are absolutely vital to have in place to make Equality of Opportunity a successful programme. We would like to think that we have developed what is a very practical approach.

Xerox Corporation & Rank Xerox (UK) Ltd

Let's begin with, a few key facts about the organisation. We employ about 100,000 people world-wide. Our annual revenues, including Xerox Corporation, are around US$19Billion. In the United Kingdom, in our sales, marketing and technical service organisation of which I am a Director, we have around 5,000 employees. Our annual revenues in the UK are around US$800 Million.Xerox Corporation/Rank Xerox are represented in every European country, and in virtually every country in the world. We consider that we are truly an international company.

Our lifeblood is product innovation. We are the organisation who started a unique industry from the invention of the Xerographic Copying Process. The industry was ours, but over a period of about twenty years we managed to let great deal of it slip through our fingers, although we are now fighting back.

The name Xerox is synonymous with innovation. We have had a series of excellent ideas that sometimes we have exploited well, and others we have not exploited at all. Our business now is Document Management.

The backdrop to this presentation is an organisation in the process of change - significant change. From reprographic to office systems, from printing systems to electronic publishing, from system reprographics to facsimile - the whole technology of our business life is changing.

Our Core Values

Now let us get on to the real core of our organisation and our values. We built our Equality Opportunity Programme around six basic core values. Ones that I think you will recognise and hopefully can associate with.

First, and most importantly we can only succeed through having satisfied customers. It is our number one business objective, and the focus of our minds always. We need satisfied customers to grow our business.

Second in priority - but in reality equal first - is the fact that we value our employees. We value the self-esteem of the individual, and achieving a balance of diversity within our organisation. We believe that to achieve satisfied customers, we need satisfied, motivated people. We need employees who actually *want* to work for our company.

We have a history of Quality. We try to deliver quality in everything we do, be it a product, a technical process or a programme to encourage more women into management. We really do try hard to get it right first time.

As an organisation we are hard on ourselves and very much into making money. I guess in industry today making money is sometimes a dirty word - not in Rank Xerox. It is the reason for our existence. We require a premium return on our assets. It is one of our core values.

So when we assess a programme, we look at the way it will add value. We are not a philanthropic organisation. We had to convince ourselves that the Equality of Opportunity Programme would give us greater returns for our business.

We use our technology to deliver market leadership. By that I mean we work hard to make sure that our products support our drive into the marketplace. And, as a European Company, we work hard at being a responsible corporate citizen. We believe that is not enough just to take, we have to add something back into the markets and the countries in which we work.

Rank Xerox (UK) Ltd

Let me now break down that figure of five thousand people in the UK. Around two thousand are professional support staff with five hundred and sixty in management. A further fifteen hundred of those five thousand people are actually customer service engineers. And a further

700 are sales executives. You can see that a minimum of two thousand two hundred are in daily contact - a prime interface - with those very important people, our customers.

Now let's look at the number of women that we have in our organisation. I am sure it will come as no surprise to you that something like 60% of our professional and support staff are women. With customer engineers the situation is very different. Of 1500 service engineers only 0.5% are women. In sales around 15% are women, and in management it is about 14%. As an organisation I do not think we are particularly atypical in the numbers of women that we have in these categories - whilst proud of our achievements through our Equality of Opportunity Strategy we know we have an awful lot to do yet!

Equal Opportunities is a Business Priority

We believe that equal opportunities has become a business priority. We are seeing the style and the culture of our organisation beginning to change as well. If you had to characterise Rank Xerox, we were run along military lines in business terms - command and control. Now we are moving away from that style. We are moving towards an organisation where individual and team empowerment is the way of the future. We are moving from an organisation where technical advantage meant market share, and market success to an organisation where it is the quality of the employee in addition to the technical quality that sets a company's products apart.

During this transition we came to recognise that our customer base is diverse. Diverse as individuals and in the way that they bought our products and needed service and product support. If you want success in the marketplace then you have to change with it. Again it goes back to that point I was making earlier on that this is not just a programme in a social sense, it has become a programme to drive the success of our organisation.

We were also moving away from what we call 'company focus' to a focus on the value of the individual. 'Balance' is a word I will be using a lot in this presentation - where the focus is on the organisation *and* the individual. The company no longer 'owns' you as an individual. Now your individuality is recognised, it is your right.

Our objective in Rank Xerox is to create an environment where individual differences are valued, and where there is balance. Where people come together as individuals to form teams. Where the individual contribution is fully recognised and valued, but the collective output of the team is also valued and seen to be greater than that of the individual. We believe that to be successful we need to create project teams drawn from different cultures, styles and experiences, coming together as units to move our organisation forward.

Our objective is to create a Company where everybody can aspire to their full potential. That is not to say that we see everybody wanting to become a managing director. Some people are quite happy to be service engineers, they look for the technical challenge in life - they don't want to be anything other than service engineers. But our objective is to make sure that, whatever an individual's aspirations, we have the programmes, styles and cultures to support them getting there.

We are completely convinced that Equality of Opportunity, including our women in management initiative, completely supports our business objectives. It dovetails very closely with the sort of organisation we want to be, and gives us something very valuable - competitive advantage - in two significant ways. One is through widening our skills base by having a wider pool of people to choose from, and the second is optimising individual contribution. We call it 'valuing diversity'.

Valuing Diversity Increases Customer and Employee Satisfaction.

With our changing culture and new skills we see ourselves delivering better services and products. If you go back to those values I talked to you about earlier on, we could see that by driving all this change we can improve customer's satisfaction significantly, and customer satisfaction is competitive advantage.

As I also said earlier, Rank Xerox was described as white, male, young and boisterous. Well, unfortunately you cannot stay young for ever. If you want to stay with the organisation you grow old, we are growing older as Company. The other thing that doesn't change at the end of the day is our focus on success.

What has changed is due very much to the influence that Valuing Differences can have. We are developing a new pool of people to choose from. We can actually see an organisation where people do value individuals - perhaps not the traditional Rank Xerox individual - and opportunity growing through that.

The organisation values the individual, raising your self-esteem rather than just sucking you into it. We are seeing productivity and creativity coming more to the fore; we are seeing ourselves becoming more innovative as an organisation through having a different and diverse culture.

Finally, we are seeing employee motivation grow, step by step, year by year, as we actually make these programmes live. All are driving towards greater competitive advantage.

Changing the Paradigm

If we look more closely at the paradigm change we are going through it is has parallels in society. We see the two coming together. We believe that our traditional attitudes and some of our assumptions and practices have held us back significantly. We believe that encouraging women into management as part of our Equal Opportunities Programme will actually liberate many new opportunities. It will drive our strategy of change. As it liberates potential, it will liberate the creativity of all our men and women. We believe that this sea change, the shift from the traditional to the future, is absolutely vital to our success as a corporation.

What I would like come onto now is how we are actually changing our culture. How did we challenge what was a tightly defined and highly successful organisation culture?

Cultural change is often associated with risk and fear. When you have been successful, both as an organisation and individually, then there is reluctance to let go. Good reasons why this sort of cultural change is so hard to effect, and why you need so much time and energy to make it happen.

One of the most important things we did to start the cultural change process was first to obtain what we call 'vital status' for the Equality of Opportunity Programme. In Rank Xerox any programme achieving this accolade is highly valued as one of the most vital programmes that we have in our organisation. As a vital status programme we have a dedicated Programme Manager - someone known to many of you - Viki Ford. Equal Opportunities, including women in management are now on the lips of an awful lot of people.

In Rank Xerox this programme will not suffer the fate of one that comes to the forefront briefly but at the end of the day, when the going gets tough, becomes of secondary importance. In Xerox we see Equality of Opportunity, including women in management, as essential to our core business. We see it as a programme that really we have to make work if we wish to succeed in the Nineties. So we made it a mainstream programme. We also integrated it into our existing business processes in terms of the review and assessment process. I will talk more about this later.

Measurement is vital. We find it is not enough just to say we would like to do it, it is not enough just to encourage people to take part in it. We actually inspect, measure and check each individual to make sure that really they are supporting it - they are doing what they say. We work very hard to make sure that people at Rank Xerox 'walk as they talk.'

Let me take you very quickly through the building blocks that we felt were essential to our success in terms of the highlights. Then I will go back to talk about the details and how we started the programme.

Top Level Commitment is Essential

We knew that to make this programme work, top level commitment was vital. First we took our role models, our Board of Directors, and took them through an equal opportunities workshop. Second, we went into the whole process of communication of information. Before getting into the detail you need to make people receptive to, and aware of what the complete programme is about. So we organised equal opportunities workshops for all 5,000 people in the organisation. We gave everyone the opportunity to learn what the Equal of Opportunity Programme could mean for them. We will talk more about this in a moment.

Finally we had to reinforce their understanding of the culture change and the new policies, programmes and practices that would sustain it. Let me now focus in some detail on the equal opportunities workshop we held for our Directors, which in itself turned out to be a fairly significant task. In Rank Xerox, probably as in a lot other organisations, the Directors are usually the people that drive change. From our equal opportunities workshop for the Board of Directors, we sought five basic outcomes.

First, to increase the Directors' breadth of understanding of the programme. Secondly we were looking for their commitment. Thirdly we wanted them to come up with a vision of the future and to begin to model the organisation into one where Equality of Opportunity was a vital programme. Fourthly we were actually looking for their permission - I use the word advisedly - for this programme to live, to reach a decision to act, and finally for them to support the long-term culture change.

I was part of that equal opportunities workshop some years ago. I remember very clearly going through the debate and discussion - and at the end of the day we achieved a commitment to the start the culture change. In Rank Xerox as elsewhere, getting the Director's commitment is critical.

Let us move on now to look in some detail at how we communicated information on the programme. We wanted to 'brand' equal opportunities just like we brand everything else in our organisation. We wanted it to be a 'product.' To this end we devised our unique equal opportunities strap line 'We Only Discriminate On Ability,' that has rapidly become an important by-line in Rank Xerox's advertising, literature and in the way people think. It has become a living phrase. We also moved equal opportunities forward by talking about it through in-house magazines. I think advertising people call it trying to drive a subliminal change - opening people's minds to the idea of equal opportunities and what was going to be a very significant cultural change.

We already had an equal opportunities policy. One of the first things was to update it, refresh it and make it live for people. We held extensive communication meetings to raise people's understanding to a common level on how it would affect them. We tried to take out some of the fear that was beginning to bubble at that time. We also carried out some research and analysis looking at the policies and practices internally as well as some external benchmarking. We became involved in what was going on - not only related to our particular business and marketplace - but in other organisations, and like companies in other parts of Europe. Also we tried to understand the real needs of people in terms of equality of opportunity, and the types of projects we might actually start. We believe that the diagnostic phase is very important indeed.

Communicating the Change - Workshops for All

Turning now to the main thrust of organisational change. Obviously the main communication, the main part of the understanding process was the equality of opportunity workshops. All of our 5,000 people went through an intensive one day workshop programme over a two years period. It was a pretty tough programme. Their format was similar - whether a managing director or the guy who drives the truck. I use the word 'guy' carefully because most of our organisation at that point was men.

During the workshop programme we flushed out some sceptics, found several cynics and unearthed many bigots. We are working hard to change them. Now, I think in life you have to accept that you will never change everybody. We accept that. But, as the organisation and most people started to change, peer pressure begins to isolate those individuals not prepared to do so, to give it a chance, and they started to stand out.

What was the main result of our workshops? We had an 80% favourable response. Bear in mind this was the first time, except for our cascade of Leadership through Quality programme some years before, that we had ever run this sort of workshop programme for all. Individuals said it was the best programme we have ever had, the best programme we have ever experienced. We need a change and we can see the logical business benefit in this programme. So the organisation was starting to move. This was the key accelerator to change.

Building Ownership of the Changes

Individuals felt part of the programme. They felt involved and able to carry it forward. They had a common understanding. One of the unanticipated spin-offs of these 450 plus workshops days was that we ended up with a whole series of very valuable recommendations, and superb ideas that the individuals and teams actually created as result of those workshops. 5,000 plus ideas worth exploring, 5,000 opportunities to enhance and capitalise on equal opportunities in Rank Xerox.

Important to our continued success with what was now becoming a very successful programme, was really equal opportunities policy number three. A programme of change and a policy that was actually driven by the outputs of the equal opportunities workshops. A policy that for once was actually owned by our people.

New policies were developed around maternity absence - outputs from the workshops and inputs from mothers.

There were also new policies on career breaks and flexible working. In Rank Xerox it was macho to work long hours - if you didn't put in twelve hours a day, six days a week, you were considered a wimp. That was the sort of organisation we were. Now we are starting to value individual output and contributions. We are actually accepting that people have different requirements and needed different work patterns.

I will give you some examples of these changes. We have annual hours contracts. We now have people job sharing. In one of the organisations that I look after - the Customer Response Centre in Milton Keynes - we have a husband and wife job sharing. One does two days a week the other three and it works very well. We have part-timers. These are cultural changes and practical approaches in support of equality of opportunity for women and men that we could not actually have envisaged or accepted five years ago. We also developed a new policy dealing with sexual harassment. We are aiming at creating an environment where women and men feel valued and respected.

We have tried hard at increasing the number of women in our service force. Even now it's not high but five years ago it was zero. I think we all understand the problem of attracting women into what has been traditionally a technical male environment, it's very difficult. We are also targeting our recruitment advertising to attract more women sales executives. We have set goals in terms of women in management.

142

We are taking part in the Opportunity 2000 initiative and Rank Xerox is now a Target Team Member. We have done an extensive study on child care and are looking to making it a live issue in the organisation.

Monitoring Progress - Walk as You Talk

Individuals within Rank Xerox have roles, responsibilities and objectives that are reviewed during a twice-yearly appraisal process and that actually style and focus the organisation as individuals and teams. We have built equal opportunities into those roles and responsibilities. We have made it a day to day process, a day to day practice.

We also focus hard on succession planning and as part of that process to bring ethnic minorities and women into management - new individuals and groups of people that traditionally we would not have done.

Each year we carry out an Employee Satisfaction Survey of all our employees. Part of that survey process, is to ask people's opinions about the Equality of Opportunity Programme. We also encourage, in fact require, our managers to carry out management practices surveys. We know from our experience that you need a certain style, you need a certain culture, to make equal opportunities live in your organisation.

The Board of Directors reviews progress towards our women into management goals quarterly. We look at the trends versus goals. We measure our progress by function. Naturally, not every function has the same goals. But everyone has to report on progress and, if unsuccessful, identify what plans, processes and positive action they have in place to actually strive toward their goals. We treat the measurement and inspection of our Equality of Opportunity Programme just like any other key programme that we have in our business. We make it really live.

What Have We Achieved?

First, let us look at women in management. We were at 10% in 1990 and now we are at 14%. Our goal is 25% by 1995.

Second, women returning from maternity absence. We developed a new policy targeted at getting them back to work. We were at 25%, now we are at 80% and our goal is 100%. Now you are going to say you will never achieve a 100%. You are probably right, but if you do not aim for it you will not come near it.

Next, the number of employees on non-standard contracts - a real indicator of cultural change. We had two, now we have 75, and we also now have a philosophy in the organisation that says: where the individual and the business needs meet then we are quite happy to go along with it. The percentage of women as new entrant sales executives was 10%, now its 20% and our goal is 50%.

Finally, our annual percentage intake of women graduates was 20%, (most of them probably in human resources), is now 25% and our goal is 50%. We are making significant progress. Success does build success.

So, if I can summarise. We are talking about culture change; we are talking about moving people's minds; we are talking about asking people to open up and forget the past. It's a very difficult change to make, tough to implement.

I think resistance in the organisation is inevitable. Resistance from individuals is also inevitable. The latter is often harder to spot, but it is there and still needs to be addressed.

We believe in Rank Xerox that top level commitment is essential in driving things forward.We also believe that the review and monitoring process are vital to make sure that people were walking as they talk. Finally, this is not a short-term programme. It's a long haul involving much change.

I would like to leave you with this final thought. Rank Xerox 'Only Discriminates On Ability'. To that we would add 'we are no longer the Company we once were, nor yet the Company we want to be'.

PART FIVE

The Barriers to Equality

Irresponsible Fathers, Long Working Hours and Executive Prejudice

Scarlett Mccgwire, Journalist, Author & Media Relations Consultant

Scarlett Mccgwire is a freelance journalist and media relations consultant. Her book:'Best Companies For Women' was published in February, 1992, by Pandora. This shows that, even in the most enlightened UK companies, few women are making it to the top.

A former President of the National Union of Journalists, Scarlett Mccgwire has written two other books.

I am the author of a book published recently entitled 'Best Companies for Women'. I would like to share some of my principal findings with you.

In order to collect material for the book, I sent questionnaires to the several hundred companies that I discovered in my researches had been contributing in any way towards encouraging women to develop their careers. Things such as enhanced maternity leave or childcare provision. They were not necessarily outstanding examples, I simply contacted any organisation that seemed to be doing something, and from which I might be able to assess better the state of play for women in Britain.

A Big Gulf Between The Best And The Rest

The most interesting outcome was learning how much the very good companies were doing. In some ways, reading the questionnaires and interviewing people gave me a too rosy a view at first. One woman after another eulogised about such things as getting promoted while on maternity leave, and sundry other successes.

Soon I came to realise there is an enormous gap between those at the top and the rest. In many companies there is still a minimal recognition of the fact that women do have children, and do actually need special facilities thereafter. Many provided only the minimum maternity leave possible, forcing women to go straight back into a full time job without recognising that, if that happened to be in management, demanding a 60 hour a week from a new mother was actually not good for business.

Retaining Women Makes Sound Business Sense

What I did find was that those companies who were the best were not necessarily more altruistic, but in fact they had understood that providing equal opportunities made business sense. It is very important to get the message across that it is financial madness to hire women and then let them leave when they have children. Often this not because they do not want to return to work but because they don't want to return to the sort of incredible hours that are expected of them.

But let us go back one stage. If you are in a highly skilled industry that is actually looking at recruiting women it is an established fact that, amongst science graduates for example, the women graduates are extremely good, even though they may be small in number. The oil and the engineering companies both said to me at interview that, on the basis of qualifications and performance at university, they found women were often superior to men, which is why they were recruiting them.

Once you have recruited women into these industries where they received skilled and costly management training then it made sense to ensure you retained these women to obtain a good return on your investment.

Local Government - The Best Employer For Women

Perhaps unsurprisingly, the best category for women that I came across was local government. Here, because of the lower pay levels, local authorities will quite often put up good packages for women, for example on extended maternity leave. They will also train people. This can be incredibly important - not just at a management level - but more especially at the lower end where an awful lot of the women have left school at 16 or 18 and later will need training to achieve their highest potential.

Also ahead was the retail services industry, as you might expect with eighty percent of women, the good companies being Sainsburys, Marks and Spencer and Littlewoods - the latter having been in the equal opportunity business for 20 years.

Also finance, again needing to do a lot as they rely heavily on women. However, in local government, finance, and retailing I have to say that women have still not reached the top, even with an 80% representation level. Indeed, most women remained at, or near the bottom, but they were still trying.

The real surprise to me was how good television was for women. Thames Television, London Week-end TV and the BBC, which was good just about everywhere not just in television, and Yorkshire TV which was trying hard. However outside London the television companies were not nearly as good. People are always knocking on the doors of television companies. Every job at the BBC, even for a secretary, yields masses of applicants. Whereas finance and retail need to attract women, and local government, television certainly doesn't.

Oil Companies Are Also Excellent

The other interesting industry to me was oil. Oil companies to me did not equal with 'good news' for women. It seemed to me before I got into it that oil was similar to engineering, very male dominated. And oil companies certainly are male dominated. But a third of the graduates recruited by BP, Esso and Shell are now women. It's an awful lot if one considers how few women graduates are reading, and graduating in the sciences.

It's only been happening for women in oil over the past ten years, so I cannot actually tell what is going to go on at the top. I will come to the "glass ceiling" in a minute, but certainly women up to the early forties are doing well in the oil companies. There is no question that the oil companies are very generous on maternity leave. BP, Shell and Esso all offer women returners part-time work, some women work from home. Although we are not talking management here until very recently, part-time work was basically for women in sub-management jobs.

Now it's changing. Because management jobs are very stressful, involving very long hours for most women, with young children it would be impossible to mix the two. But to my surprise the oil companies were very sympathetic to women who, for example, want to work from home three days a week, and come to the office two days. A senior tax advisor at Esso comes to work three days a week following the birth of her child. She wants to change it to five mornings when the child gets older.

Is It all Good News For Women?

So it's all good news for women, at least it all seems to be good news for women. The best companies are certainly doing an awful lot for mothers. That's where the concentration is. Finally they have recognised that they cannot let them go and in order to achieve this they must do something about it. A surprising number have, but not as many as one would expect from reading the newspapers. Places like the BBC have creches, although Broadcasting House where BBC Radio is situated doesn't have one.

Obviously creches actually don't solve problems for a lot of people. Creches have very strict hours but if you're working long hours they are hopeless. For a lot of management women they don't answer the problems at all.

Creches take a lot of money, and make an obvious show of commitment by the company. However, what shows more commitment is instituting flexible hours. Companies like London Week-end Television have also given extra money to woman returners and, above average maternity leave. When all is said and done the government minimum is pretty dreadful!

So there is a greater encouragement to go back to work. There is obviously a recognition by the better British companies that women do have an awful lot to offer and that they cannot let them go.

Few Women Have Made It

The bad news comes in my book when one looks at the statistics of women in senior management. Women in middle management are not great in number, but we are getting there, and in some companies women in junior management have reached 50%. But for women in senior management, women as directors and women on the board, the percentages remain minute everywhere whether it be Sainsburys, the oil companies or in television. And outside the good ones they are absolutely non-existent.

I interviewed 150 women for my book. Some of them said: "I think I am going to do it, I think I will break through the glass ceiling - I don't see what's going to stop me". An awful lot more of them said "well this place is alright, it's fine for me at the moment, but I don't know what I am going to do in five years time, because I can't see me breaking through into senior management".

This is a terrible problem for women and for industry, because it is a complete waste. I feel that industry is crazy to believe that half of the population is not up to senior management. Frankly, some senior male managers are just not good enough to be keeping a lot of excellent women out.

Some places have recognised this. Mars for example is targeting women into management. The reason being they feel their culture is too macho. It was very interesting to discover that they felt there was something wrong, that women were not being promoted in the same numbers as men. But they also felt that you need a decent number of women managers, not just tokens to show that they can do it, but enough women managers so that no one woman is carrying the weight of all women in the company on her shoulders. It has to be normal for women to be out there. They feel that it might be patronising, they feel that women will bring a different flavour.

Now I don't know whether this is right or wrong, there are a lot of theories about it, and most of them are only theories, because there are not enough women in management yet to show if we make a difference. Certainly a lot of the senior women I spoke to were up there on their own, Most good engineering companies did have a very senior woman. She was usually alone and often felt that things would be very tough until other women were up there as well.

However, all the women I spoke to were very certain about one thing. They did not want positive discrimination. They wanted people to know that they were up there absolutely on merit, because they were the best. There was no question of anybody wishing to be promoted because they were a woman.

This was a very common sentiment, not just among senior women but also very junior. There are other ways around it, like proper training and looking to see what is wrong with the promotion process if women are not getting up there.

The Glass Ceiling And Childbearing Are Synonymous

I have three theories why all of this is going to have to change. There is no questions that the glass ceiling occurs about the time that women have children. That is when it all stops. In theory it seems that there is everything to play for. And I remember thinking to myself that the women out there just did not get it right. We can all do it, we can work long hours, we can do everything that there is to do. And then one looks at women over the age of 35, and suddenly the men are racing ahead and the women are falling behind.

And so it's obviously about having children for most women, I do think that women should not have to choose between a family and a career. Nobody ever asks a man if he has small children and how he's going to cope with the new job or the promotion. For many women it is a real problem, and this is why one of the keys to women getting on is actually fathers, men.

Fathers Must Take More Responsibility

Nothing will change until fathers take more responsibility for their children, in the same way that mothers do. Until fathers have actually to think about sorting out the nanny and what's going to happen when they go away on the business trip, and what will happen when a child is ill, i.e. which parent is going to take the day off?

It is these things that we have got to change because, as long as fathers do not have to take action, there is a double discrimination. One is the mother of their children has to do everything. They have to do the juggling and keep up their career. The other thing is that if you are in an office with fathers and mothers, the mothers are always seen as the problem. I mean a father is not a problem because he is not doing anything.

Actually all of us have got to make sure that if we have children the fathers of these children do things, not for our sake but the sake of the women they are working with. Because when it becomes parents who have to do things there will be so many parents that maybe employers will lose their prejudice against families.

Long Hours Are Unnecessary And Discriminatory

The other thing that is terribly discriminatory is hours. Most of the women I spoke to in management work incredibly long hours, 60 to 70 hours a week seemed to be quite normal. Obviously what a lot of them did was work 8 to 9 hours at work, they then came home, put their kids to bed, they gave them supper, bath and then as soon as the kids were in bed they got out their work again, and worked until they went to sleep. It was just incredible.I think that one should look at these hours and "say is it really necessary and how long can one go on doing it?"

In the Health Service two senior job sharers now run a Health Authority. One of them started job sharing before she had children, she was doing seventy to eighty hours a week, and she felt that she never had time for anything else. Although she was running a hospital and felt she was doing a good job, she could never stand back and try to plan. As a job sharer she feels that she is much more efficient, even with a much

153

more senior job, where she formulates primary care policy as well as running the health authority.

I think we should have a future in which being successful does not mean giving up the rest of ones life. Because actually getting ahead and having prospects should mean getting better at working, being more efficient. The other reason of course why women don't get ahead is because there is an enormous prejudice against women from senior levels. Senior men can find successful women frightening.

What is amazing is that women spend their time being told it's their fault, they don't push themselves enough, they are far too shy, they will never do it, etc, etc. Suddenly they are at the top middle management level and men find them too aggressive. We are talking about a lot of senior men who have a wife who does not work. It's a different sort of culture, they are used to have women to look after them, that's the way they see it, and suddenly they have those women who want to be up there at the board room with them and they don't like it.

A Three Point Cultural Change Is Necessary

How we change that culture I don't know, but change that culture we must. One television managing director was saying to me that he did think that it was just a matter of time, he's quite young, did not go to public school, and has a working wife. And he said that he does see it changing, and there is no questions that some of the prejudice is going.

In my experience, in newspapers - I am not going to name names - but I can tell you that most of the editors of quality newspapers have problems working with women, they really do. I mean they find it difficult to have serious conversation with a woman. And I am sure that newspapers do not attract the worst men in the world. I am sure that other companies have their problems too.

So those are the three things I think we really have to sort out: fathers, working hours, and somehow, the unease of senior men with women. Then I think we can really go forwards.

Caring is the Real Issue for Women

Anne Watts, Equal Opportunities Director, Midland Bank &
Christine Lyles, Manager, Equal Opportunities, Barclays Bank

Anne Watts is a Commissioner of the Equal Opportunites Commission, and numerous other management groups and associations, including the National Womens' Enterprise Agency and the Development Target Team of Opportunity 2000. She is Equal Opportunities Director of Midland Group.

Christine Lyles is a lifelong employee of Barclays Bank, holding a number of appointments in the personnel area before becoming Manager, Equal Opportunities in 1986. Christine Lyalls is a member of the Institute of Personnel Management.

Anne Watts: Banking has had both women and equal opportunities for a long time now, and many of the topics which have been brought up in the previous presentations have either been discussed, directed, or monitored by both our organisations. We will be introducing what we feel is a qualitative issue - how you make these things happen in companies, and what are the real issues for women in business organisations?

Women form a very important resource in banking, in fact they comprise the majority of our staff. So the first issue is not one of access - we have been accessible to women for a long time now. The real issue for women in banking is how do they move up the hierarchy, and what are the barriers and difficulties that they face?

The first thing that we want to look at is balancing needs. How do we balance those of the individual against the business? How can both sides profit?

Women in Banking

Banking is a traditional industry. In the UK as a whole it has over 350,000 staff - so it is a large employer - with women comprising 61%. But as you rise up the banking hierarchy you can see that women disappear quite rapidly. The mass of female employees are clearly at the lower end of the scale.

Why did we feel the need to act?

Our first consideration was the age profile - women are staying longer and moving further up the grades. Second, the whole issue of maternity and the low return rate. Third, the fact that there simply were not enough women in management anyway, which any customer can see just by walking through our front door. Demographic change also played a part - even though some of the emphasis varies, the underlying trends remain constant. Equal opportunities is also a vital business issue.

Let's now move over to Christine Lyles. Both our banks took part in the National Cares Survey and she is going to tell you about the results.

The National Carers Survey

Christine Lyles: With women comprising 65% of Barclay's employees we had to understand what the principal issues were if they were going to remain in our workforce and climb the promotional ladder.

In 1988, as part of the on going development of our equal opportunities programme, we took part in The National Carers Survey. The survey was designed to find what caring responsibilities people had, both men and women, how they managed those responsibilities, and what they needed from their employer to help them find the balance between work and family. The survey was very important for us. It involved a cross-section of our staff and the following were its major findings.

Whilst half the staff have caring responsibilities, many of them have dual responsibilities and, of course, both men and women are affected. Around 65% are caring for children, no big surprise, but to find 38% caring for the elderly was unexpected, as was the fact that over 70% of our respondents also told us that they expected that their problems were going to increase. Of course, we do have an ageing population and, therefore, an ageing workforce and we must consider the Government's policies on care in the community which will come on stream in 1993.

Better Understanding and Greater Flexibility

When we asked our staff what they needed, top of the list for both men and women was flexibility of work time arrangements, and simply better understanding and recognition of their problems and, of course, the lack of affordable childcare in this country was another major issue.

We now had to establish a business case to bring about change within the organisation, and in the case of Barclays a closer look at our workforce profile was seen as the key. We found that changing gender ratios had significant implications for us.

The preponderance of women used to be concentrated in the clerical grades when they left us for childbearing, and were relatively easily replaced. Now it was quite different. Over 40% of our senior clerical and supervisory grades are now female and comprise the pool from which our future management will come. Over the next five years or so over half of them will take a maternity break, and many of them will ask for the part-time working option that our career break scheme offers.

Realising that we really *had* to make some changes in the organisation in order to retain those women, we felt that we had to go to our line administration managers who were going to be the ones who were going to have to answer this call for greater flexibility.

Our staff told us very clearly what they needed, and so we formed a working party of line administration managers, and they came up with a list of flexible working arrangements that we in the Equal Opportunities Section developed over the ensuing months.

Examples of Flexible Working Arrangements

Job Share Contracts: We developed this policy, piloted it in a couple of regions, and now it has been introduced across the country. We see job sharing as a way to facilitate part-time working in the higher grades in the bank, with management jobs being shared in the future. Term-time, contracts are also now available and used where the business need can accommodate them.

Emergency Leave: This gives anyone the right to take up to five days leave without notice in order to cope with those emergencies we all face from time to time.

Carer's Break: This was designed for those people who faced a long term responsibility - caring for an elderly dependant relative, or a partner taken seriously ill. It allowed for a complete break for up to six months, or six months part-time if, for example, arrangements could be made for a district nurse or something similar. These staff have the right to come back at the same grade and keeping all benefits, such as housing loans, intact.

Of course, if the problem is not resolved during this period then we have built into the policy the idea that a member of staff can either continue working permanently part-time or, if they have no alternative but to resign, they may stay on a reserve list with us and come back in the next two year period.

Banking and Borrowing Holidays: This was aimed at staff wanting an alternative to taking the current year's holiday or taking unpaid leave. We have introduced borrowing holiday, and we are working on the banking idea at the moment.

Maternity leave: We felt we could manage more flexibility there, especially for a second child, and we have introduced an extra three months that staff can take, and maintain all of their benefits and, of course, the right to return at the same grade.

Home working: We are trying out a couple of pilot schemes. This is very new, but I do see that in the future this is going to be another avenue for flexibility that we will introduce into the organisation.

The Benefits of Focusing on Childcare

Anne Watts: Childcare was an area that Midland focused on. We felt that it was of such great importance that we should find out exactly what was happening. We established that the average cost of replacing one women going on maternity leave was equal to the cost of their employment in the year preceding. The average cost of maintaining one child in a nursery, however, is far less than that and therefore there is a significant benefit to be gained both by the organisation and the individual from instituting nursery places, and nursery provision.

Currently we have 116 nurseries open to us offering 810 places. We have also established 60 holiday play schemes We are still looking at other forms of provision, including after-school care although some of those areas are not easy to define.

The return from this investment over the last three years has been a rise in the number of women returning from maternity leave from 41% to 73%, and I am quite sure that it will continue to rise.

All in all, will it make any difference? Well, we are beginning to see that the numbers of women in management are moving up, so if you are hoping to see still more as senior branch managers then continue to watch this space!

Apprehension and Inertia in Electronics

Kevin Kennedy, Chairman & Managing Director,
Philips Electronics UK Limited

Kevin Kennedy joined Philips Electronics as MD of Philips Telecommunications and Data Systems in 1986. He returned to the UK in 1990, following a spell in Holland, a s MD of Philips Electronic and Associated Industries.

A Council Member of the CBI and Fellow of the BIM, Kevin Kennedy's leisure interests include golf, music and reading.

My job today is to give you a perspective of the situation of women managers as seen from the viewpoint of just one industry -Electronics.

I will confine myself to talking about women managers, or those with managerial potential. The role of women in industry as a whole is a massive subject, and I could not possibly say anything meaningful about it in the time available.

Let me start with a word of warning - one addressed to myself rather than to anyone else. What I do not intend to do is to tell any woman - or man - what she or he is, or should be thinking. I want to give

160

you some idea of the future requirements of our industry, look at some of the career aspirations of women and link the two.

Women in the Electronics Industry

I have to be honest and say that in the electronics industry we have very little to shout about. As is well known, we employ a very large number of women - in Philips it is around forty percent. However it remains a stark truth that very few of them are at, or very near the top. There is not a single woman on our main board, or our supervisory board, and in Philips UK women account for less than ten per cent of our management group.

Indeed, when it was known at Philips that I was to make this speech one of our female managers commented that she was sure I would not go through with it. In twenty minutes or so you'll know if I should have listened to her advice!

Bearing in mind that 'people in glass houses should not throw stones', I will not. I am not in a position to flaunt any credentials - or tell anyone else how to do it right. What I am in a position to do, after thirty years in this industry is to look at how its requirements are changing.

I then propose to ask how much the needs of women meet the changing needs of the industry. I shall also discuss what we as an industry should be doing about it. I should emphasize that any solutions I propose are for industry to execute - nobody else.

The lack of senior women managers in our industry seems strange when you think of our customers Although my own company is involved in integrated circuits, medical equipment and communications technology - as well as consumer electronics - the vast majority of our products end up in the home. Given that the majority of buying decisions for the home are made by women why are they not more involved in the decisions about which products these customers will buy?

Part of the answer is that electronics is a business where invention is the mother of necessity. Our industry has always been driven by research and development, production engineering and, yes, the occasional flash of real inspiration. That means that until now the trick has been 'keeping up with the Joneses' in product development and engineering.

An industry with this structure has historically been managed by engineers and production people. They have tended in the past to be men. Women have, by and large, not run production units. Whether this is because they have chosen not to - or not been chosen - is a moot point. This is a fact.

Our Markets and Technology are Changing

But things are changing - and changing fast, both in terms of technology and markets. Let me take technology first. New production technologies are altering the balance of employment. A modern automated production plant may have only a tenth as many workers producing the same output as before. Production management today relies more on computer techniques than old fashioned expertise in metal bashing.

At the same time potential managers of production plants in the future are emerging through the traditional route of an engineering degree. One of the few bright aspects of the generally grim outlook for skills in the last few years has been the steady increase in the numbers of women taking professional engineering qualifications. This is creating the potential for more women to move into management positions in areas that have traditionally been almost exclusively a male preserve.

Global Competitors and Market Driven

But the change in the external environment of business may have even more impact. We have discovered that engineering is not all. The problem with invention being the mother of necessity is that you then have to create the need for your invention.

There is no point making the best new product in the world if the world does not see the need for it. No one knew they wanted a Walkman till Akio Morita invented one. In the same way Philips now has to convince consumers that they need the combined benefits of a home computer, television hi-f and video library, by selling them the interactive compact disc.

All of this is compounded by the radical changes in the way we are doing business. The electronics industry is now in global competition for markets. As protectionist barriers vanish, businesses are under ever greater pressure to shorten research and development times, and bring products to market to an ever- higher standard and in an ever-shorter time. If you wished to sum up the new environment for business, it would be that while the risks are huge, the rewards - and the penalties for failure - are immense.

The industry, in common with other consumer businesses, is now market driven as never before. The resultant shift in the balance of power is away from R&D and production engineering towards marketing and the relationship with the consumer. The electronics industry is coming to terms with this sea change.

Philips, as you may know, has launched a major programme aimed at changing the way we think as a business - and orienting Philips more towards the needs of the customer. The culture of industry is changing. With this greater emphasis on meeting the needs of the consumer, companies are investing more at the points where they meet the customer, and less on internal administration. This has involved redeploying resources - and as a result, redundancies.

What Kind of Managers are Required Today?

Some of the resources saved are reinvested in marketing and customer service. Let me pause for a moment and try and draw up a balance sheet. What impact have all these changes had on the sort of managers the industry needs?

I start with the bad news: bad news that is felt by everyone, male and female. Managers today work a lot harder and a lot longer hours then they did a decade ago. Competitive pressures mean that jobs must be finished in a much shorter time. And today's manager does not just work longer hours - more of those hours are away from home. With the internationalisation of business, there is much more overseas travel than there was in the past. I am sure I am not alone in wondering if these long hours of work will continue to produce better results over the long term. To my mind, a tired manager rapidly ceases to be effective.

But there is good news too. Today's managers are much less stodgy and status-obsessed than in the past. Some symbols of exclusiveness of yesteryear - the separate washrooms and the managerial restaurants - are disappearing. I am not sure that all managers have woken up to the real culture changes that go with this.

Today's manager needs to be much more flexible and change- oriented than in the past. He - or she - must be a good listener and a good communicator, must look outwards not inwards, must be proactive not reactive. Today's manager is much more participative in style, combining the role of team coach and playing captain. Team working, joint effort and good lateral communications are much more important than dynamic leadership from on high.

The reason is simple. A company that does not have a culture of joint effort and commitment to certain values is a company that will fail. Managing this change of culture is stressful, and calls for a strength of character and purpose that is not taught in most management schools. It may even require a completely new breed of manager, with different values and a different background.

The Qualities and Needs of Women Managers

Many of the characteristics of the modern manager outlined above could be found just as well, and possibly better, in female managers as well as male ones. In support, let me quote a recent article in Business Magazine: 'Women bring to business a set of values, a level of commitment and a willingness to act on intuition, which today's businesses need'.

All of which brings me back to the potential role and perceived needs of women. To put it simply, I believe that many of the demands on new industrial managers matches the demands of potential women managers. My evidence for womens' attitudes comes from my own experience, published survey material and from interviews with women managers at Philips. I do not claim these as representative of anything other than the views of those who took part. At best such surveys indicate general trends.

There can be no doubt that most women feel that their job potential is not being realised. This is not individual paranoia because the vast majority of women in work state that their relations with their male colleagues are good or excellent. Most accept the pressures I was talking about earlier, and work very hard. A Cosmopolitan survey of 3000 readers published this month supports me in this.

What Holds Women Managers Back?

So what then are the blockages stopping this keen and energetic group of workers from improving their positions? I think that the two major factors involved are apprehension and inertia. Any management appointment carries some risk. Given the choice between appointing a man or a woman to a management position, the appointment of a man is perceived to be the lowest risk option. His appointment does not bring any unfamiliar risks or requirements. The appointment of a woman may. I wonder if some women do not also share this perception - as women do not have a good track record of appointing other women to management positions.

The same perception problem exists when looking at who should receive what training. This is arguably where a major part of the problem begins. In the survey I just referred to, most respondents begged for extra training opportunities.

When we talked to women managers in Philips most said that the training they had received had come as a result of pestering their seniors, which brings me to the subject of inertia. Several members of the group also cited prejudice of an unintentional or informal kind. They acknowledged that there was concern at this within the company, but the point they were making was that this concern was ineffectual.

All agreed that they had progressed as far as they had because of lucky timing, being in the right place at the right time, and - most important of all, having a fair minded and forward thinking boss early in their careers. I guess that most men would say the first two factors were as important for them also. The third factor however, is the real bar to women. Male managers have to start thinking differently, and understand the business reasons why we can't continue with current attitudes.

Let me turn now to another, much quoted, barrier. Much has been said and written of womens' desire for flexibility at work: job sharing, extended maternity leave, career breaks, flexitime and the like. In the past such demands were regarded as a nuisance, and as damaging to the smooth running of a large company. I suggest that no one would dare to say that sort of thing today: but equally that very few employers yet take the subject seriously. Only a quarter of employers in one recent survey offered any possibility of job sharing, or flexitime or any extended maternity benefits. To be blunt, many company programmes in this area look dangerously like tokenism.

Let us look at this from the viewpoint of women. I have already mentioned the high degree of commitment to work - that features in a number of surveys. There is also a strong belief that women can combine motherhood with a career: in the case of the Cosmopolitan survey, 98% believed that. With one important proviso - that they had a supportive employer.

Dealing With Unintentional Prejudice

I would now like to come back to what I believe to be the real barrier, the one that I mentioned earlier: 'unintentional or informal prejudice' and what do we do about it?

I will start with a basic point: but one that nonetheless I feel bound to make. Despite the recession, every company I know is crying out for good managers, and, perhaps more important, for people with good managerial potential. More especially they want people who can adapt to the changing circumstances I have tried to outline.

If we had decided that on some purely arbitrary basis we would only recruit managers from half of the male population then you would rightly say that we were not fit to run any business. Without getting into any debate about equity, not accessing the female population of our employees effectively, which we do not, is a business mistake equally stupid as not accessing half the men.

We have threatened the future of our businesses in this way not, I suspect, because we were deeply prejudiced, but because we were, and are, uncertain. As I said earlier, men have been frightened of taking 'apparent' risks.

Industry has tended to corral its women managers into a very small number of areas: ones which were felt to be - and I put this in quotes - 'soft' areas. Departments like personnel, administration, public relations and education - oh yes, and marketing. Now from what I have said earlier, you will realise that marketing is fast becoming a 'hard' area - again I put it in quotes. Marketing is now in the mainstream of most businesses. It is also encouraging in my own company to see how many new product design teams are now led by women.

Male Attitudes Must Change

But that is only a start. Male managers must also change their attitudes. I return to the connections between the needs of industry and the desires of women managers. In our discussion with female managers at Philips, we found that they felt under-appreciated for the real assets of personality they had. Phrases they used about themselves included: and I quote them directly 'no ego problems', 'liked by everyone', 'more sensitive on many issues', 'better at getting things done'. I have read an awful lot of job advertisements that could with profit have included those phrases.

So why are we not doing anything about it - or are we? The answer is a bit like the accuracy of the weather forecast: patchy. Some companies are making a major effort. At ICI the numbers of women moving into middle and senior management positions have trebled in five years - and the same is true at Barclays Bank. But while acknowledging efforts like that, one must remember the starting point.

Affirmative Action or Voluntary Change?

A much greater effort needs to be made. I believe we need affirmative action. What is at issue is whether we need affirmative action backed by law. The United States of America has had that for some years, and it's achieved some results. The European Commission is considering it.

I would counsel caution, while agreeing with the principle. The problem will not go away with a quick legal fix. If I may put it in psychological terms, a human being functions at three different levels. On the surface there is a day to day behaviour; beneath that there are a set of attitudes which influence that behaviour. While right in the middle of the onion there are basic values, which in turn ultimately determine the two outer cores.

You can change behaviour by law - I think of the seat belt law as an outstanding example. It is much more difficult to changes attitudes. As we know, attitudes change slowly over a long period of time, and attempts to change them forcibly over a short period of time tend to fail. Fundamental values on the other hand are very difficult to change.

We could enforce positive discrimination on employers. I suspect the results would be ultimately counter productive, because of the hardening of incorrect attitudes that would result. After all, those women in whose favour there has been positive discrimination have to function and work closely with male colleagues who, by implication, have been discriminated against. I suspect that most women managers would hate to feel they were there because a law said they had to be.

I believe that the answer lies in a voluntary change of behaviour patterns, leading to a gradual change of attitudes and - who knows - eventually to the adoption of new core values. That has to come from the top in the form of leadership, a word that I have rather consciously avoided so far with all my emphasis on team making and consensus.

Why do I say it must start at the top? Because, if Chief Executives have one important thing to do in a modern business, it is to set the agenda for corporate behaviour - whether that be in relation to competitors, investors or employees. It is a job which cannot be delegated.

Changing Behaviour and Attitudes

When should we start? We have - but we need to go faster. We cannot Go on ignoring the needs of a vital section of our potential employees for many more years, pleading that it is 'a problem'. A problem is only an unrealized opportunity. We must start looking at things the other way round and start on the hard slog of changing first the behaviour, then the attitudes.

We have a long way to go. Even in those companies which have made a major effort, the percentage of women in management grades has only now reached around 10%. I do not want anyone to think that it is a matter of one big effort to catch up.

There is no such thing as catching up - whether in this area or any other area of running a large scale modern competitive business. You cannot catch a river. But you can swim with it - and the clever manager is the one who manages to swim downstream faster than the river is flowing. Managerial white water rafting may sound odd, but that is what I am talking about.

Well, where should we start then? A few companies have put figures on their ambitions, perhaps a little rashly. But it is something that has to be done even if numerical targets do not suit every case. I would suggest a more modest ambition for those reluctant to jump in at the deep end. We could try and retain a larger proportion of the few senior women managers we already have. The drop out rate in many companies is depressingly high, much higher than for men. Cut that back a bit and you will find that you have started to solve the problem. You will have created a valuable aspirational role model for other women inside the company.

The most important thing to bear in mind in any programme of affirmative action is the advice from Corinthians: 'The Lord loveth a cheerful giver'. Don't do it because you ought to, but because you want to. We must take our own internal affirmative action not because we are frightened of being caught out or think the law will chase us. We must take positive action because there is a positive reason for doing so.

If for no other reason, I think we must do so because where women lead others will follow. The demands that women are making today for flexibility, independence and opportunity in the pattern of work - is becoming more widespread. Who knows, even men may be saying publicly the same thing? If for no reason other than survival, we have to realise that new patterns of working are coming.

An Action Programme

To sum up. Any programme for action must be directed at two different areas: actual company practice, and managerial thinking.

In the field of practice, companies must set themselves real achievable targets - they may not be easily achievable, but they must be achievable. These targets must include better retention levels, and a clear statement of intent on numbers of women managers in the future and why.

In Philips, as I mentioned earlier, we are currently going through a major change process. Part of that is an examination of the management skills and attitudes we believe we need on an international basis in the future. Our initial conclusions support the comment I quoted earlier about the values and behaviour women bring to a business. And you will see that reflected in what we do.

The other area - managerial thinking - is more difficult. Most male managers have accepted intellectually that we can't go on as we are at the moment. I do not think they have yet accepted the idea emotionally. We have to look closely at the reasons behind the apprehension and inertia I talked about earlier. Men will be helped in this difficult task if women articulate their needs more clearly.

In short we must get away from the polite niceties of management-speak - or the megaphone - and talk to each other. We must find out what male managers are really frightened of - and what women managers really want.

I said at the beginning that industry did not have much to shout about. But we could always start with a little bit of quiet talking - and even more, listening.

The Fear of Change

Sir Bryan Nicholson,
Chairman and Chief Executive, The Post Office

Sir Bryan Nicholson was Chairman of the Manpower Services Commission and Rank Xerox UK Ltd, prior to joining the Post Office as Chairman and Chief Executive.

A member of the National Economic Development Council, Sir Bryan Nicholson also chairs the Council of the Industrial Society and is a Vice President of the National Children's Home.

Sir Bryan has a long term interest in education and training.

I suppose a Euro-Businesswoman Conference has three strands - Europe, Business and Women. I do not propose to add to the first. So much has been said and written about Europe in the run-up to 1992 that I feel that there is little that I can add. What is certainly true though, is that the days of the famous newspaper headline are long gone. You remember it? 'Fog in English Channel: Europe isolated'.

There are certainly things that I could say about business, but I am not sure that this is the time or the place. No, I would rather spend time talking about the role of women in business, and offering just a few personal observations.

171

You would be hard pushed to find a representative of any reputable organisation who would be willing to make a statement against the need for equality of opportunity. Indeed, most of them would be able to run through some of the basic arguments which are deployed in favour of a policy of equal opportunities. The spread of recognition of the need for equal opportunities, not simply because of the economic case that can be made, but because it is the right course to take for its own sake, is one of the most encouraging features of business life over the past few years. It was not ever thus.

One of the biggest barriers which has been overcome in the acceptance of equal opportunities as an important goal for any business is that of fear. There are now enough role models to persuade the faint-hearted that they will not lose by encouraging more of them to join their organisations. Indeed, there is plenty of evidence that such a policy provides positive benefits to the organisation, and is instrumental in providing the best human resource base for the work it has to do.

I am particularly proud of the role the Post Office has played as a founder member of Opportunity 2000. Our involvement in this initiative has provided a fresh focus for us in ensuring that equality of opportunity is an integral part of our business action planning process.

Top level commitment is all very well, but it butters no parsnips. The French novelist, Balzac said: "Equality may be a right, but no power on earth can ever turn it into a fact". I like to think that he was wrong, but accept that there are times when the distance between the policy and reality is distressingly wide. What I would like to look at this evening is how that distance can be reduced, or removed, so that policy is implemented effectively and willingly. The challenge is to stop merely paying lip service to equal opportunities, and bring about action.

Equal Opportunities - Getting the message Acrosss

Let me say straight away that I do not think that the problem here is unique to the implementation of equal opportunities policy. There is always a time lag, not to mention a distortion effect, between the formulation and implementation of policy, and any organisation, particularly a large one, faces difficulties in avoiding this. The further removed a

policy becomes from its source - typically the higher levels of the organisation - the more it is prone to be delayed, modified or simply blocked
by those in the organisation who do not share the same aims.

There are a number of lessons for us here, but let me look at just
two - communication and organisational structure. In both cases the
messages are fairly obvious, but nevertheless of great importance. Messages on equal opportunities need to be clear, unambiguous and directed
at the right people. Lukewarm support for vague principles is not good
enough. If leaders do not lead, how can anybody be expected to follow?

Similarly, the right messages need to be effectively communicated
directly. Passing the word down lengthy chains can so often lead to a
surprisingly different message emerging at the other end. Look again at
those chains of communication. Why are they so long? How many lay-
ers must your equal opportunities policy pass through before it can be
implemented? How many people get the chance to put their own gloss
- or their grubby fingerprints - on it before they put it into action?

It is no coincidence that so many successful companies have
stripped away layer upon layer of management, looking at the value
people add rather than the empire they control, when measuring their
worth to the organisation. There is a great deal about equal opportunities
that is not really different from other business issues, and it is sometimes
useful to bear this in mind. One such feature is that responsibility needs
to be focused in the right part of the organisation.

Centralisation or Devolution?

No two organisations are alike, but the fundamental choice which
needs to be made is whether prime responsibility for equal opportunities
should rest centrally, or be devolved down the organisation. The right
balance needs to be struck between centralised power and local accountability. I am by nature a devolver. I do not believe that it is sensible to
develop a mighty headquarters which holds all the strings, and plays the
organisation like a puppet.

In the Post Office in recent years we have made conscious and
continuing efforts to give power to managers at the lowest level consistent with proper control, thus making them responsible for their own

destinies. At the same time we recognise that there is a need for a degree of centralised co-ordination to ensure that each wheel is invented only once, and to act as a custodian of best practice.

The Post Office is a particularly large organisation. We turn over around £6 billion per annum and have 220,000 people on the payroll. There are separate and distinct businesses dealing with letters, parcels and counters, so there is an equal opportunities function in the headquarters of all three businesses, as well as in the corporate centre. There are, though, only a handful of people involved in headquarters, and the primary ownership of equal opportunities rests at local level. The role of headquarters is to establish and promote policy; implementation in different local circumstances is down to the people close to the issues.

Equal Opportunity Policies in the Post Office

The Post Office, in common with most large organisations, has an equal opportunities policy, and indeed it has had one for a number of years now. I would not claim that it is either better or worse than the policies established by other companies and organisations, but it does provide the terms of reference within which equal opportunities are implemented. The policy aims to eliminate unfair and unlawful discrimination, and to promote equality of opportunity for all Post Office employees, and indeed for job applicants. Some years ago the Lady Mayor of Ottawa was heard to remark: "whatever women do, they must do it twice as well as men to be thought half as good. Luckily, this is not difficult".

I am very pleased to say that our most recent internal survey shows that this is not a view shared by today's women managers in the Post Office!

Earlier I mentioned the need to overcome the barrier of fear in implementing equal opportunities policy, and I'd like now to return briefly to that theme. I think we have to accept that although there is a significant amount of enlightened goodwill helping the cause of equal opportunities, many people still have attitudinal difficulties. Attitudes are notoriously slow to change. They are private, personal emotions, developed over many years and reinforced by evidence carefully selected to fit the bill. They do not change overnight. New language has to be learnt, and that can be a painful process, particularly for older people, and may even be used as an excuse to reject the principles involved.

Training and Motivation

Training, and particularly awareness training, is important but does not provide the solution on its own. Indeed, use of appropriate language may actually lag behind the adoption of new ideas, so it is worth making sure that you don't ignore real commitment on the part of an individual who happens not to use the most acceptable phraseology.

People need to be motivated to change, not forced or coerced. Never is this more important than when their efforts have apparently failed. People need to learn that there is no magic short cut to achievement. Decades of malpractice simply cannot be undone by a couple of weeks of honest endeavour. It's sometimes hard to understand that after years of being rejected people take some persuading before they believe that a change has come. Behind every success story in the field of good implementation of sound equal opportunities policy lies chapter upon chapter of hard work, frustration and more hard work.

Ultimately that hard work will bear fruit. There are enough organisations now who provide excellent role models of what can be achieved to give encouragement to everybody else. I think that they would agree that they did not suddenly stumble across the solution,and blinding flashes of light do not happen for many people. They have achieved what they have by steadily exerting pressure for change at the right time, and in the right place. I have been particularly heartened by changes I have observed at grass roots level in recent years.

From time to time I take the opportunity to meet with groups of graduate entrants who have recently joined the Post Office. For several years now the groups have been around 50/50 young women and young men, a most satisfying reflection of the proportion of graduates leaving our colleges and universities.

Another example of change I came across was a year or two ago when I was in Munster in Germany. There local polytechnic equivalent is in a European consortium of higher education institutions with, amongst others, Humberside in Northern England. There I found young women and young men in roughly equal numbers from both countries studying international business together. Truly the Euro-managers of the future and something largely unknown even a decade ago. I wonder if perhaps more is already changing at grass roots level than we realise.

Total Upheaval as a Last Resort

I do not advocate total upheaval as a method of progression unless the situation is so rotten that there is nothing to lose. It is often possible to use a subtle shift of emphasis as a method of changing the whole style and angle of particular systems. Let me give you an example. It is often said that recruitment by word of mouth is discriminatory. Not necessarily true. It depends on whose mouth has been the vehicle for keeping certain types of work within a confined group of people, and thus being discriminatory. If a company becomes known as one with an enlightened attitude to equal opportunities, and gains a reputation for good practice, recruitment becomes a far simpler issue.

How does its reputation get known?

By word of mouth. The old system can be adapted and used to meet new needs. Businesses need to become more imaginative in their approach to issues such as working patterns if they are to develop this type of reputation. There will always be constraints in certain types of time-critical occupations, but where possible we need to do more forward thinking in adapting our large corporations to provide an environment where we actively encourage and support women - and men - in balancing home commitments with an interesting and varied career.

This should not simply be an expedient response to demographic change, because that implies that the commitment could be dropped if no longer necessary. The recession has gone some way to defusing the famous demographic time bomb, but it would be a serious mistake to ignore those many keys areas where skill shortages remain.

Neglecting Potential is the Real Crime

More fundamentally, it would be unforgivable, in my view, to neglect the potential of a group of people who form over half of the population - women. Let's not forget that so-called 'minority' groups actually constitute a majority.

But majority or minority is not the point. The point remains the full and equal use of all the talent available in a business. That is now accepted wisdom if not applied practice. Bridging that gap requires perseverance and perhaps the key message is to persevere.

It was once said that "the drop of rain maketh a hole in the stone, not by violence but by oft falling". We must ensure that the drop falls often and in the right place.

Male Chauvinism Slow to Die in Advertising

Danielle Barr, Chairman and Chief Executive, Publicis

Danielle Barr headed the advertising operations at the Natwest Bank, prior to joining McCormick Publicis as Managing Director in 1987. She was made Chairman and Chief Executive in 1991.

A council member of the Anglo-French Chamber of Commerce and the Marketing Group of Great Britain, Danielle Barr has also spent time working with Goya, L'Oreal and Elida Gibbs.

Before I get onto the subject of recruiting and retaining women in advertising, I would like to spend a couple of minutes talking about advertising in general.

Advertising is a little different from the professions and industries covered in this conference, for the simple reason that the product of the advertising industry, i.e. advertisements, in their many forms pervade everyone's life. Whilst some would rather use the word 'invade', others quite enjoy these little intrusions, which offer light relief between depressing news programmes and predictable soap operas. In fact, in the

UK, 75% of people actually like, or at least do not mind advertising, and only 25% object to it. In America the reverse is true.

So advertising is an accessible, easily understood, often entertaining, commercial tool. Clearly, it is an effective tool, that is worth using. How else would one explain that £Nbn was still being spent on advertising in 1991 in the UK during a recession when advertising budgets have been severely cut!

A great deal of this money is directed at women, particularly television advertising. It is worth remembering that television advertising started by selling mass market, fast moving food and household products aimed exclusively at housewives. It was only later that cars and airlines and now computers and sportswear started using TV targeting men as well.

Does Advertising Encourage Gender Stereotyping?

Another relevant aspect that makes advertising rather unique is its portrayal of women. This is a huge subject and raises many important questions, such as whether advertising uses stereotypes e.g.:

— Are women portrayed as sex objects, moronic housewives or superwomen?

— Does advertising reflect society?

— Should it reflect attitudes or attempt to shape them?What about gender roles when advertising to children e.g. dolls for girls, cars for boys?

I do not intend to delve into these issues but I wanted to underline the fact that by being a potent persuasive tool, the actual product of the advertising industry can influence the view women have of themselves and their capabilities.

But advertising is a commercial instrument, not a social engineering tool. Advertising is used to achieve commercial objectives, and is evaluated using commercial criteria. As such, it tends to reflect society and its attitudes rather than lead them. Having looked at advertising, and advertisements, we need to look at the advertising profession as well.It is actually very small and shrinking.

Women in the Advertising Industry

There were 13,000 people involved in advertising in September 1991, working in 245 agencies, compared with 14,800 people in 275 agencies in September 1990 - the recession has certainly taken its toll - and since September last year there have been more lay-offs in which women have not been spared either as we shall see. But overall advertising is a good career for women to enter. Prior to the recession half of the people entering the profession, mostly university graduates, were women. However, there were very few women at the top of agencies.

So in 1989 the new President of the Institute of Practitioners in Advertising (the advertising agency's trade association in the UK) felt that the time had come to look into the matter.

He asked Miss Marilyn Baxter, Director of Planning at Saatchi & Saatchi, to undertake a study which would identify the reasons why there were so few women at the top of IPA agencies and to make recommendations to improve the proportion of senior women in advertising.

Marilyn used the advertising industry's own skills to carry out original research and explore the underlying attitudes and reasons. She developed a number of hypotheses before reaching the view that there was no single cause or solution. The situation in advertising, as in so many other walks of life, is the result of a matrix of interlocking forces - sociological, historical, biological and economic.

One of the ironies of the situation is the forthcoming shortage of young people of employable age entitled by Marilyn as: 'Manpower And Recruitment In The Lean Years Of The Nineties'. What we did not know at that time was that the lean years would affect everyone, not just the young.

Because there was already a high proportion of women going into advertising the study concentrates more on retention than recruitment. Nevertheless it was as detailed, comprehensive and self critical as any industry has carried out into its own policies and practices with regard to the employment of women.

Women Managers in Advertising

The survey showed that while women are farther ahead in advertising than in many other industries or professions, we are still a very long way from having achieved equality, and further still from an acceptable situation. Nevertheless, as I already said - advertising remains a good career for women.

Women have made far more progress in our industry than in most others - but they still accounted for only 14% of the directors on agency boards, and there were only 22 female chief executives and managing directors in all IPA agencies in 1989 and there has not been a rash of appointments since then!

Women's success in advertising varies greatly by job function. They are most evident in planning, research and media and - somewhat surprisingly - least evident in creative departments, with only two of the top 50 agencies having women as their creative directors. Probably the single main reason for the under-representation of women at the top is that 15-20 years ago comparatively few were recruited. Twenty years ago only 19% of graduate entrants were female. Today it is 45%.

Additional factors appear to favour men. These can vary from department to department, but long working hours, maternity and childcare, the male ethos of agencies, some client prejudice and lingering male chauvinism among agency managements play significant roles in impeding women's progress.

However, it is clear that by no means all women working in agencies wish to make it to the top. Some do not feel advertising to be a sufficiently 'worthwhile' job, while others reserve the right to leave to become mothers and housewives. Many women lack the confidence to push themselves forward. Those that have achieved success in agencies consciously play a variety of roles, adeptly juggling homes, families and careers. Ignoring prejudice, they minimise male attention on 'feminine problems', like managing a family and a job. But a generation gap is already appearing here. Younger women reject such artifice, feeling strongly that it is unnecessary.

Recommended Improvements

So this is what the survey into the advertising industry has revealed. But, as mentioned, it was not intended merely as a report on the existing situation, but to go further, and make recommendations for improvement. Two key areas were addressed:

— Agency managements should ensure that their practices conformed to Sexual Discrimination and Equal Pay Legislation, rejected minor discriminatory actions, dealt positively with sexual harassment, and handled maternity leave and return to work with greater sensitivity.

— Second, to increase female representation on all IPA bodies and committees, to investigate the possibility of an all industry creche in London, and to monitor womens' progress in the industry and publish the results.

Womens' Progress Has Been Hit by Recession

What progress has been made? In the intervening period since the report was published the advertising industry has entered, and remains, in its deepest recession. A recent census of the IPA agencies shows that while the total number of people working in advertising has shrunk by 12% the number of men fell by 11% but women declined by 14%. The fact that male secretaries also shrank from 31 to 10 is small consolation.

Particularly worrying is the fact that, after a steady increase in the proportion of women executives from 29% in 1987 to 39% in 1990, by 1991 this has dropped back to 36%. Whilst probably no different from other industries and professions, it represents a severe setback that will take a long time to recoup.

In fact a survey carried out towards the end of 1991 by one of the recruitment agencies found that women were losing ground on two fronts - employment and pay. And to add insult to injury it has been reported that sales, marketing and associated companies are adopting a deliberate policy of positive discrimination, not in order to encourage women - but to cut costs. Employing women in top positions is apparently more economical as they command lower salaries!

So am I to leave you with the depressing thought that even while the going was good for women in advertising in the good years, it is not good now and may get worse?

Well, I did not choose the advertising profession because I am a pessimist. As the founder of Publicis in France, Marcel Bleustein Blanchet, put it well when he said: "That's probably why I chose advertising, it embodies a philosophy of optimism".

A Ray of Hope?

There is a little ray of hope and, as is often the case it has to do with young people. Despite the recession, despite the setbacks, despite positive discrimination which turns out not to be positive at all, young women are still entering the business and the proportion of young women under 30 is growing. Not a world shattering development, but an acknowledgement that it is still an attractive profession.

What other progress can be reported?

The IPA explored the viability of an industry creche but concluded that the actual participation in such a scheme will be quite low and even though private companies would benefit from the tax relief, agencies say that the legislation is too tough to set up schemes of their own.

Not surprisingly the more senior working women are, the easier it is for them to handle the pressures of career and motherhood, but it is hardly a matter of 'having it all'. If you are on £30,000 a year, a nanny will take half of your pay after tax and with no tax relief in the wages you pay her. But even though we are not likely to see an industry creche in the near future, the IPA is showing willing by helping with information about child care facilities by commercial and voluntary organisations.

Male Attitudes Slow to Change

As for the atmosphere within the agencies - there is a growing awareness among men that chauvinism and sexist behaviour are no longer acceptable or tolerated. But we still hear of men who openly say that they prefer not to work alongside women because they would not be allowed to swear, talk about sex, cars, or Queens Park Rangers. Well, of course they are perfectly correct about Queens Park Rangers!

A final point to mention, which differentiates advertising from many other sectors is the opportunity available to women inside the profession regardless of their academic qualifications. In many industries the stance for career women is: "Don't let them know you can type or take shorthand".

In advertising this is not the case. Very many of the women now in senior positions entered the business as secretaries or assistants in the production department. Being a secretary actually provides an extremely good grounding for the job of an account handler. The combination of ability, likeable personality, luck and lethal ambition, has propelled many a secretary into the boardroom. And this is not a route available to most men.

At the start of my presentation we looked back into ancient history to see how advertisements mirrored the role of women in society. Even today we can still see examples of patronising sexism, but now it is much more common to see women portrayed in ways we would recognise ourselves - either in the boardroom or the bedroom. This is the example we are setting for today's generation of advertising industry entrants.

Lacking in Self-Belief

Patricia Vaz, General Manager, BT Payphones

Patricia Vaz joined BT in 1975 and worked in a variety of roles prior to taking up her present appointment as General Manager, BT Payphones in 1990.

Patricia Vaz leads a team of 3500 and manages all the day to day activities of BT's payphones business throughout the UK; plus three other groups in charge of strategy and operations development, product development and centralised operations.

My presentation today identifies the steps that have been taken within BT to encourage and facilitate the advance of women, particularly within the management ranks, and what still needs to be done by the Business and by women themselves to establish their position.

Firstly, I need to introduce myself and explain my background and present role within BT. I joined BT in 1975 as a clerical officer in Personnel. Very quickly I became interested in the core of the telecommunications business. My first management job was in this discipline in 1978, and was followed soon after by promotion into the marketing

185

field, where I product managed the implementation of the first stored programme controlled customer switches on the market in 1980.

In 1990 I took up my current role as General Manager, BT Payphones. I manage BT's entire pay phone business with a staff of 3700 covering the UK. Our functions range from strategic planning and business analysis, to highly qualified technical specialists developing the product portfolio, and field technicians implementing and maintaining the service. The pay phone business has a turnover of £400million per annum - significant even in the context of BT.

Women Managers in BT's Workforce

Over the period from 1975 to date, I have seen many changes in BT's approach to women in the workforce. The development of Policies to encourage equality cover: equal opportunities; Sexual Harassment Guidelines, a network of equal opportunities advisors within the Divisions; and a statutory grievance procedure to deal with any issues that may arise. We have also amended the terms of employment to provide for: flexitime; teleworking, part-time working; and job sharing; all of which have helped women balance having a career with the demands of a home and family.

On the development side BT have also put in place a number of initiatives aimed specifically at women that include: a Cranfield course for personal and professional development; a womens' bridging course to provide technical training for would-be women engineering managers; a womens' network has been established for mutual support; health care initiatives and modules in the CORE management training package aimed at women.

BT is an excellent employer, and the efforts the Company has made continue and have indeed been re-emphasised with its participation in the Opportunity 2000 initiative discussed yesterday. But how successful have we been in encouraging women, particularly to venture into the management ranks?

Relatively Few Women Managers

In December 1991 BT's statistics show that, although 28% of our workforce were women, only 16% of these were managers. Relatively not too bad an achievement. However, the balance of women in management gets progressively smaller as you go up the scale - ranging from 17% in the junior management ranks to only 7% of senior managers. What is probably even more significant is that very few of those senior women managers fill general management, operational roles. As yet the only woman on BT's main Board is in a non-executive capacity.

So why is this when the steps that have been taken should have enabled a far greater proportion of women to have reached the higher levels of management? Well, as other speakers at this Conference have already pointed out it is far more to do with the attitudes, behaviours and the culture of the company - and in that I include women as well as men - than it is to do with prescribed policies and processes.

Respect for the Individual and Team Working

In its participation in Opportunity 2000, BT is reviewing its effort to encourage women by focusing on two of our key values: respect for each other as individuals, and working as a team. As our Chairman has stated in launching our contribution to Opportunity 2000 - "The essence of good teamwork at any level in an organisation is finding the right balance of experience and expertise (in BT) we have to extend genuine encouragement to women so that they feel accepted and valued as team members".

We will therefore be focusing not only on the procedures and practices already in place, but also on tracking the attitudes and behaviours within the company. We will be extending the development opportunities for women within CORE training, with development courses for women in non-managerial and senior managerial roles - but you cannot legislate for attitudinal change.

ı **Must Achieve a Critical Mass**

he only way you will really change attitudes and behaviours
ı any company is when the number of women achievers forms a
critical mass. Once it becomes the norm for women to be represented in
significant numbers at all levels of the Company, then the culture will
no longer be an issue.

So how do women get to that critical mass? There are two ways
forward in my view - we could opt for real positive discrimination
which I am totally and utterly opposed to on the grounds that it debases
the achievement of women in the long run, and could be damaging for
the company if people are not appointed on merit.

The other way is to get more women to want to get on. The enablers we have put in place in BT so far have made it easier for the
women who are already pretty determined, and as such would probably
have made it anyway even if - as in my own case - the enablers had not
been there. The key then is how to get more women motivated in the
first place to exploit their potential. After all, look at the skills exercised
by the vast majority of women in the family environment. Women have
traditionally : balanced budgets, acted as coach, kept the peace, balanced priorities, developed people and created teams. Why when we
come to work do we think that we cannot exercise those same skills in
a business environment? Or why do we think that we have to act and
behave like the men in order to gain credibility?

We are, in may respects, our own worst enemies. We have tried to
stifle the innate characteristics of women - emotion, femininity, the ability to empathise, the ability to listen, and we have through womens'
liberation actually deliberately rejected the courtesies, the acknowledgement that we are different from men. Being different can and does
add value within a team environment and within a leadership environment. Perhaps I am alone in the view that by taking this stance we have
damaged our ability to succeed.

I believe quite firmly that the characteristics I have just outlined
are very powerful leadership tools and, coupled with the talents outlined

on the slide, give us the ability to be extremely successful in any business environment.

Equal Opportunities - Helping or Hindering Women?

My final message is perhaps controversial - there is a danger that by putting too much emphasis on the policies and enabling mechanisms being put in place by companies, we are providing crutches which will help to propound the myth - because that is what I believe it is - that the system is against us. Women have to believe in themselves first and foremost - if the enablers help them to build that confidence then they are worthwhile. But if you think that policies and procedures and cultural initiatives can in themselves change the situation, then we are fooling ourselves.

The only people who can do that is ourselves and if we do not take the initiative then we cannot expect that change to occur. I would like to leave you with the thought. Is the only thing stopping women, women themselves?

The Key Issues For Implementation

The Business Professions And Trade Unions

Chair: **Professor Peter Herriot**, Sundridge Park Management Centre (Left)
Panellists:-
Susan Gompels, Council Member,The Institute of Chartered Accountants;
Jean Irvine, Chair, Women Into Information Technology;
Lorraine Paddison, Vice-President, The Institute of Personnel Management;
Margaret Rutherford, President Elect, The Chartered Institute of Arbitrators;
Gareth Williams QC, Chairman of the Bar Council;
Simon Wilson, Trades Union Congress.

Chair: I am going to ask each of our panellists to say in one sentence what they believe to be the key issue for implementation that they have heard in the course of today.

Simon Wilson: Taking a national perspective - because I come from a national organisation - targeting is fine, but turning best practice into common practice, turning the business case into the national case, requires a framework of legal rights, and also some attention paid to collective bargaining.

Susan Gompels: A great deal has been laid down in the way of frameworks, and enabling system within organisations. Women now have special responsibility where they can be seen as role models, and should be aware of the immense impact that they may have both for good and for ill. People must be encouraged to believe in themselves, to undertake personal strategic planning, and set their own clear targets. Thus prepared, women should also take more initiative to push open those doors which are now ajar, helping others through as they do so.

Gareth Williams: People in positions of authority must stop talking in platitudes and demonstrate commitment. We have sixteen committees on the Bar Council under my chairmanship - nine of which are being chaired by women. Actions not words, let's stop talking generalities.

Lorraine Paddison: This is a business issue. It has to be approached and managed in exactly the same way as any other business issue. Our final presentation from Lucas summed that up extremely well in terms of setting clear objectives, action plans, targets, and accountability. That is what we have to do.

Jean Irvine: I think essentially it is about organisations becoming total quality businesses. If you look at the management culture in total quality organisations, they value the skills and expertise of all of their employees. When they talk about empowerment of people, they mean that. The other thing in terms of key implementation issues is to introduce a little passion into strategic planning. Let's make it exciting! Because if you don't make it exciting - and this is where role models can help tremendously - to make people want to push those doors open, then we will not succeed.

Margaret Rutherford: We need continued anger, continued pressure, continued social education and continued action by our own example.

Chair: Following from your opening statements the major issue I would like the panel to consider first is translating the valuing of diversity into a business issue.

Jean Irvine: I would like to start on the subject of valuing diversity. It is about, really about, having the people doing the work in organisation having power over the decision making. Particularly in the West we have too many hierarchical, old style, male-dominated managements within organisations, keeping power and information at the top.

By having more team working down through organisations, and people nearer to the delivery point making more decisions, you will come to value different approaches. It is about giving up power and control, moving very much towards a team-working approach to management, and where many women can bring additional interpersonal skills to make businesses more competitive.

Chairman: How can this happen? How can team working become part of the culture and mode of work in the organisation?

Jean Irvine: Through leadership from the top. If you don't get the Chairman and the Board really focusing on team working, and setting task forces to deal with businesses issues, it won't happen.

Chair: Any thoughts from your colleagues?

Simon Wilson: As a Trade Unionist my perspective is perhaps a bit different. The difficulty is that everyone talks about best practice: people say this is necessary, otherwise companies will not survive. Our problem is that Trade Union members continue to work for companies that are not going to survive. And when these companies stop surviving, they lose their jobs. We cannot afford to wait for managers at the top to come down and say "we've got a strategy".

I would also like to say that some Trade Union Organisations with members in companies which signed up in Opportunity 2000 were somewhat surprised. For years and years they had been arguing about equal opportunities - perhaps using the wrong language but they have been doing it - and met resistance. Finally, one day a manager gets a bright idea in his head and suddenly all is well!

Our view is that if we are going to achieve the day when half our 'Euro-businesspeople' are Euro-businesswomen, then you have to have a decent framework of rights applying to all women, including those that are working in companies that are badly managed, so that they will always be heard. So a business based strategy is fine but it needs to be backed-up with something else.

Jean Irvine: I am not at all sure that the Trade Union movement in the UK is one of the greatest advocates of equal opportunities and diversity. Certainly I believe that much of the emphasis on collectivism has destroyed a lot of the focus on diversity, particularly in large organisations where we are now finding it extremely difficult to recognise and reward individual achievement.

This is a legacy of the fact that many trade unions working through collective bargaining want everyone to be treated exactly the same. So a lot of our equal opportunity is about identity.

Chair: Simon, would you like to respond?

Simon Wilson: I have to say that everything that has been said today is very familiar to me. However, let's not overstate this - the basic framework for maternity leave, equal treatment, fighting discrimination, opposing sexual harassment in most work places comes first from trade unions.

When you then look at the next step of greater diversity, of course I admit that in some cases Trade Union organisations can seem to be an obstacle. The thing to do is to confront us on our own terms, challenge us to take up these questions. I think you'll find in recent years there have been a lot of changes.

Lorraine Paddison: I have been very encouraged to be here today. It's been tremendously stimulating to see the rate of change, although this is a long term process. I was particularly struck this morning by senior male managers who were very positive and stated "This is good for my business and I am proud to be here to say that". Certainly that is a change. We would not have heard that two or three years ago. But what has preceded that in their organisations is some kind of change agent stimulating the process.

Sometimes it is trade unions, and quite often it is the personnel people or equal opportunities department. But essentially we have to think ourselves into that selling process, we have to help identify what is in it for the business in each particular case.

Gareth Williams: We have a sightly different perspective at the Bar because you cannot really say to an individual barrister "it's good for your business". We are all single practitioners, so the approach that we take is rather different. We have tried to encourage women to come to the Bar and to make sure they get a fair crack of the whip when they come there.

About 42% of entrants to the Bar course this year are women, which is encouragingly high. We have actually changed our code of professional conduct to make it a specific disciplinary offence, which could be lead to disbarment, to discriminate against anyone on the basis of sex, ethnic origin or religious belief. So that is something quite important really. What we say is, that if you welcome people with energy and commitment the whole profession will benefit.

Susan Gompels: At the Institute of Chartered Accountants over the last twenty years we have seen a dramatic increase in the number of women coming into the profession. Around a third of students qualifying each year are now women.

We have similar problems to some extent, to those of our colleagues from the Bar, in that equality is something to which we have to pursuade individuals, in a personal as well as an economic sense. Of course many accountants do work in large organisations in industry and commerce, but irrespective of size and area of operation, professional activities are essentially commercially based. These changes of attitude must be seen clearly as a business issue.

Certainly, when I talk to colleagues, the approach I take relates to practical project and business planning. We try to encourage the suspension of old stereotypes, and a vision beyond the traditional "twenty-one year-old, male, white, technology graduate" image!

Things are changing. We do not have to work in central London; we do not have to work between 8am and 6pm. There is a great deal of variety in the work that we do, and a totally new menu which we are trying to put in place in a economic sense, and that is where the people issues come in. The current debate over women in the work place , and women in to senior management, is in the vanguard of what is basically a 'people' issue, promoting respect for the individual in the longer term.

Margaret Rutherford: Yes, if I could just associate myself with my colleague from the Bar. I am not sure that we do not need at least a measure of positive discrimination, so that we can get at least a certain proportion of women appointed as judges or as arbitrators. I believe the Lord Chancellor has indicated that a certain percentage of appointments to tribunals have got to be female. And I am all for that. Although I take all the points I have heard concerning positive discrimination.

Chair: Shall we move on to the idea of the design of work, which has come up two or three times, and the notion that if work, and the way people work together is designed differently, then business issues will be affected and diversity would be greater value. Would anybody on the panel like to address this?.

Jean Irvine: In the technology-based business that I am in, and with all the technology we have got, it ought to be very easy for a lot of people to work from home. However, one of the thing we are finding is it is not a lack of technology that is creating the problems. We do not have the management skills to manage people who are not physically in front of us. Too much of management is about managing people's time, and knowing where they are, and not measuring their output.

So we are putting a lot of new measures and systems in place that focus very much on managing people, and what they give to the organisation. Not on how they do it or how long they spend at it.

Susan Gompels: Actually, we did a recruitment study recently and one of the aspects we looked at quite carefully was the effect of technology on our work - we have had people with computers working at a distance for some years.

We came across a number of factors in this regard. You do have to learn different management approaches. You do not have to physically see people, but you do have to learn to trust people, and this involved some fairly major attitudinal shifts. At the same time the management of distant teams has to be particularly well and sensitively done. It is not just about managing teams, as we are used to. Very often those people who are being managed at a distance suffer stress and overwork - exactly the reverse of many expectations that people will shirk if not supervised. In fact people can end up as workaholics from bad distance management.

Chair: Very interesting, a technological change making possible a new mode of working, which then require new modes of management.

Jean Irvine: Can I just respond with a cautionary tale of the continuing for management education. One of the reason we set up the Women in IT Foundation, which is a charity, was the declining number of women coming into the profession as the same time as a the huge demand for new skills for IT professionals.

Now the current recession has hit the industry very hard and most firms have stopped recruitment. What has happened in fact is that many firms have stopped worrying too much about some of the equal opportunities issues that they were concerned about before. So, whereas we had a desperate demand for returners courses, mid-career courses, etc., now we are finding that some of these have been taken off the agenda.

I think the gap that we now have to fill, is ensuring that business managers identify their business needs and future skills requirements, coupled with the need for greater flexibility and then we will find equal opportunities back on the main board agenda again.

Chair: It is really interesting that we are not talking about business issues solely in terms of their being financial issues.

Jean Irvine: But I think they are financial, because I think anyone who believes that by working fourteen hours a day they are giving value added' is kidding themselves.

Chair: Clearly I am not saying that financial issues are not involved in business issues. All I am saying is, that there are business issues which are not financial issues. An absolutely key one, as we all recognise is information technology.

If I may have the last word here, I think that information technology is just like other technology, it can be used for good or ill; it can be used to control, or it can be used to liberate. I still think it is up to each organisation to decide how it is going to use it.

Thank you to our panel for helping us conclude the conference.